THE WIND THAT NEVER CHANGES

The wind blows where it wishes and you hear the sound of it, but do not know where it comes from and where it is going; so is everyone who is born of the Spirit. (John 3:8)

I the LORD do not change. (Malachi 3:6)

Jesus Christ is the same yesterday, today, and forever. (Hebrews 13:8)

Essays on the Christian Life
by Charles H. Perry

Charles H Perry

Introduction

In February of 2002, I had a burden for the people I worked with at a major international corporation. There was a no solicitation policy at the company so I was not able to tell everyone I worked with about Jesus and His love or pass out any Christian literature during work hours. I decided to write a small book about salvation in Jesus with the intent of mailing all my former coworkers a copy to their home addresses after I retired. This I did after I retired in December of 2003. Since that time, I have used the small book as an evangelism tool like a gospel tract. "Essay I, Knowing God," is that little book. It is a basic message on knowing God through the sacrifice of Jesus on the cross. Individuals who know Jesus as Savior and Lord do not need to read Essay I if they are confident in their relationship with the Father through the Son and "know that they know" (I John 2:3).

A friend reviewed my little evangelism book and noticed that I said nothing about the importance of water baptism after receiving Jesus by faith. This got me to thinking. Water baptism after receiving Jesus as Savior is important and should not be minimized. However, many believers in Jesus are taught that sins are washed away in water baptism, otherwise known as baptismal regeneration. This is considered a work done by the believer necessary for salvation. "Essay II, Baptism," addresses this doctrine in detail. The goal of Essay II is to show from Scripture that the one baptism in Ephesians 4:5 is not water baptism after receiving Jesus, but rather the identification of the believer with Jesus on the cross and in His death, burial and resurrection.

After receiving Jesus as my savior on March 11, 1966, the Lord led me to a very sound, strongly Bible-based church that gave me a solid foundation in the Word of God. However, this church was also strongly against the so-called supernatural sign gifts such as unknown tongues, prophecy, and healing. After about 10 years in that church, I moved to New York. Initially my wife and I attended an independent Bible church similar to our home church. Over time, several problems in our life and marriage made us realize we were not getting what we needed at our present church. I had met some believers at work who practiced the supernatural sign gifts. They really impressed me with their Godly character and the reality of their walk with God. My wife and I decided to visit their church. This was the first church we had ever attended that regularly practiced the supernatural sign gifts. At first, it was very strange—holding up hands, loud and long worship, prophecies and other activities we were not used to seeing. We could not deny the presence of God in these meetings. They were real, vibrant and anything but ritualistic. So, we kept going. Over time, we came to fully embrace this style of worship and all the supernatural gifts. This happened in 1985. Since that time, we have seen the operation of the supernatural gifts as a valid expression of the work of the Holy Spirit for the present time. Having been associated with a non-charismatic church since 1966 and close associations with charismatic churches since 1985 has given a unique perspective on the activities of the Holy Spirit. For this reason, I wrote "Essay III, Spirit of Truth." My primary motive was not to strongly argue for or against particular spiritual gifts, but to point out the importance of love and unity in the Body of Christ

In the spring of 1983, I attended a weekend men's retreat. One of the speakers shared a card given to him by his wife. The front had a colorful picture of hot air balloons. On the inside it said, "Your love has set me free." The speaker pointed out in his talk that we as men of God were to learn to love our wives as Christ loved the Church and set them free from the superficial standards of womanhood created by culture. His talk spoke to me deeply. I knew my wife's insecurities and how my weaknesses had fueled her insecurities. At this time, we had been married thirteen years and had four children. For the first 11 years of our marriage, I struggled with sexual addiction that almost destroyed our marriage. While I was free from the bondage of sexual addiction, my wife still suffered from emotional wounds that were not healed.

After the session, I went out into the woods and found a secluded place to pray. I wept and wept before God and confessed my role in hurting and wounding my beloved wife. That day in the woods on my knees and weeping before God, I asked Him to let my wife say the same thing to me: "Your love has set me free." Twenty years later in January 2003, on our thirty-third wedding anniversary, my wife gave me a card. Inside the card she wrote, "Your sweet love has set me free." She had long forgotten that men's retreat and my request to God. By her own confession, she did not remember my desire, and I had never mentioned it to her again.

"Essay IV, Thou Art All Fair My Love," is the story of what happened in those twenty years and how God taught me to love my wife as He desires. It is a story of self-discovery. I discovered how selfish, proud, insensitive, and insecure I was and how to let God lead me out of the darkness of self into the light of His redemptive love. It occurred to me recently that writing my story of redemption from the power of self could reach many husbands. As an old believer once told me, "You don't have to eat the whole cake to know how it tastes." While I am far from perfect, I have "tasted the cake" of learning to love my wife as Christ loved the church. I hope by reading Essay IV the Holy Spirit will lead you to a deeper understanding of what it means to "love your wife as Christ loved the church" (Ephesians 5:25).

In these essays, it is axiomatic that God exists, that God is infinite in knowledge and power, and is omnipresent in the universe. It is also axiomatic that God had men write the Holy Scriptures by His direction, and the Scriptures as originally penned were inerrant. It is acknowledged that in up to 4500 years of copying and translating, the present day Scriptures have minor discrepancies and some minor additions. However, these minor discrepancies and additions do not alter the fundamental message of the Holy Scriptures. *God loves humans and desires a relationship with them. God has revealed His salvation from sin and death in His Holy Son, Jesus Christ.* God's message is pristine with regard to the Truth it reveals about His salvation and humanity's need for salvation. In the present day Scriptures, this message is crystal clear. To major on the minor discrepancies in the present day scriptures is just another excuse to dismiss the Truth of the Scriptures.

    These four essays were written over a period of seventeen years. Therefore, the style of each may differ a little from the others. Essays I, II, and III are on doctrine and have scripture references in the text. Essay IV does not give as many scripture references as the other three. It is a narrative of a journey as opposed to precisely-referenced doctrinal presentations as the first three essays. All scripture references are from the New American Standard Bible unless otherwise noted.

Charles H. Perry
June 1, 2019

ESSAY I

Knowing God

Before reading the essay, take a few minutes and answer the following true or false statements.
1. Most people are basically good.
2. There are many paths to God as long as a person is sincere.
3. Good people go to Heaven when they die.
4. Jesus Christ was a prophet, teacher, and good example, similar to Mohammed, Buddha and Moses.
5. We know God is in our lives because we can feel His presence.
6. Faith means believing something that is true.
7. It is enough to believe there is one God.
8. God just wants to be a part of our lives.
9. Study and meditation are the methods used to come to the correct belief about God.
10. It is not possible for a person to know they are going to heaven when they die.

The correct responses to these statements, according to the Bible, are given in this essay.

Choices

There are many events in life that must be experienced in order to achieve a degree of understanding: falling in love, becoming a parent, loss of a loved one, escape from a critical illness or tragic situation. Emotions and insights gained from these types of life events cannot be explained with words. They are deep, profound, and to a degree, mysterious. Who can explain the power of love and how it changes motives, perceptions, and actions? These changes occur in what is called the human heart. No one knows exactly what the term *human heart* means. It is a complex area of human consciousness that involves thought, emotion, and will. Will seems to be the defining element, because it determines the choices that are made in life. Will involves why certain choices are made. It has genetic as well as experience factors. It is not uncommon to look back and wonder why a certain choice was made in life. Why the human heart reacts or acts in certain ways to life events is something that cannot always be understood. We may ask ourselves, "Why did this make me so angry?" or "What was I thinking when I made that decision?" or "Why did it take me so long to realize what was really going on?" Such questions are an acknowledgment of the fact that we do not really understand how the human heart works. As Pascal said, "The heart has reasons that reason itself cannot explain" (1).

A discussion on the human heart is appropriate because it is the heart that defines and determines direction. We may not stop to analyze why decisions are made, but it is of paramount importance. Often, a critical life decision is made that will have a profound, lasting effect on the rest of our lives, and we do not even realize a life-changing event occurred. It may be years later when we look back and recognize the moment that we chose a different direction in life. When a young person decides to take up a destructive habit like drugs, alcohol, or smoking, he does not realize he has made a potentially life-altering choice. If it were possible to fast-forward that young person's life and allow him to experience the long-term effects of that choice, such as lung cancer or cirrhosis of the liver, how would he react? Would he still make a careless decision based on a momentary feeling of insecurity, rebellion, or self-gratification? The fact is that most of the time, the greatest questions of life are not given much serious thought. Why are we here? What should we do? Where are we going? *How does one live a life that will produce an enduring satisfaction and contentment?* Decisions are made every day without considering the long-term effects. We are too busy, rushed, or weary to stop and consider. In those rare moments of reflection, the reaction may be, "O yeah, that," and a few moments of thought are invested until the next crisis or urgent demand comes along. Finally, when life slows down and there is time to consider, the question is asked, "How did I get to this point?" There is a sense of loss, pain, or uncertainty when the choices made along the way were not correct after all. If the end is not fulfilling and rich with rewarding experiences, who is to blame—parents, society, God?

Certainly not God! He has made abundantly clear the answers to those seemingly unanswerable questions about life. The answers are simple and effective. Lack of knowledge is the problem. Many think they know, but their attitude and actions show they do not know. This is an essay about knowing God personally and what a personal relationship with Him can mean. This is the ultimate reason for our existence: to know Him.

Knowing God

Jesus said,

Many will say to me on that day, "Lord, Lord, did not we prophesy in Your name, and in Your name cast out demons, and in Your name perform many miracles?" And then I will declare to them, "I never knew you; depart from Me, you who practice lawlessness." (Matthew 7:22–23)

Today we might say, "Lord, Lord, don't I go to church,

The Wind That Never Changes

read my Bible, pray, and try to do what is right all the time?" or "Lord, Lord, I am always a good person and kind to other people." If this is all we could say, He would surely say, "Depart from Me, you who practice lawlessness." Why is this the case? Because He said, "I never knew you." *The issue is not what we do or don't do. The issue is whether Jesus knows us because we know Him.* "I am the good shepherd, and I know My own, and My own know Me, even as the Father knows Me, and I know the Father; and I lay down My life for the sheep" (John 10:14–15). Those who really know Jesus Christ know him as Jesus knows His Father and as the Father knows Jesus. How could this relationship between Jesus and His Heavenly Father be described? It is a relationship of divine love, which exemplifies passionate devotion, perfect purity, and absolute trust and obedience. It is an intimacy of communion, fellowship, and unity that can only be understood by those who have experienced divine love.

What is it like to know Jesus? It cannot be explained with words. The love of Jesus is greater and more satisfying than all of life's most wonderful, thrilling, and fulfilling experiences combined. It "surpasses knowledge" (Ephesians 3:19). How can one describe a stunning sunset or a breathtaking view of nature? No words are adequate for such experiences. As the song writer said, "The love of Jesus, what it is, none but His loved ones know" (2). When a person experiences the love of Jesus for the first time, there is a deep sense of "coming home." It is knowing that at last you have found what you were looking for all your life. You now have a sense of well-being and peace that cannot be described, producing "joy inexpressible" (I Peter 1:8). It is a profound realization that this is why you were created, like a bird that flies for the first time or a butterfly that emerges from the cocoon. You were created to have an intimate relationship with God the Father through His Holy Son Jesus Christ. Nothing in life can satisfy that longing. *Until we are satisfied with Jesus, we will not be satisfied with anything.* If we truly know Jesus, nothing else in life even comes close to the joy and fulfillment we have in our relationship with Him.

The most important question in life is, "Do you know Jesus Christ, and does He know you?" If you do know Him, you "know that we have come to know Him" (I John 2:3) and have His assurance of His ownership and Lordship over every aspect of your being. You also know that you have assurance of eternal life with Him forever. In fact, you already have experienced eternal life, for it is a quality of life that can be lived here and now for those who know Him. Is your life characterized by "righteousness and peace and joy in the Holy Spirit?" (Romans 14:17) Does the thought of Jesus bring forth a heart response of sweetness in joyful recognition and familiarity because of your deep and real relationship with Him? Or does the thought of God produce uncertainty, confusion, or even fear?

The knowledge and love of God cannot be obtained by any human effort. This personal, intimate relationship with God cannot be learned or taught. Human intellect is not capable of understanding this, no matter how gifted. It only comes by direct revelation from God Himself to the human spirit: "For I neither received it from man, nor was I taught it, but I received it through a revelation of Jesus Christ" (Galatians 1:12). The will, emotions, and intellect participate. They are necessary but not sufficient. Only God can draw a human to Himself and reveal to that human what He wants him to know and experience. If you are reading this, it is by Divine appointment. God wants you to come to Him so He can reveal Himself to you. Do you want to know God and be known by Him?

Worldview

What do we believe? Why do we believe? How do we believe? The answers to these three questions form something that has been called our worldview. This is the framework from which every decision in life is made. Everyone has a system of beliefs. From childhood our belief system is developed by parents, relatives, guardians, teachers, society, friends, and life experiences. As we grow, our belief system becomes more complex, and emotions become related to our beliefs. Often, the emotion associated with a certain belief is much stronger and more influential in our thoughts and actions than the actual belief itself. In many cases we would be hard pressed to explain logically why we believe certain things. This is especially true when it comes to beliefs relating to God. Often the beliefs concerning God are more associated with feelings than knowledge. The problem with this condition is that our belief system about God should be the foundation for all our beliefs. If this foundation is based on feelings, it is shaky, not well defined, and lacking a solid and rational basis. Under these conditions, the rest of our belief system and our whole life suffers.

The tragedy of a fuzzy, inadequate belief system lacking a solid foundation is that you can live all of life without knowing that there is a problem. Suppose human beings didn't have eyes—that society and technology had developed over thousands of years with no one ever being able to see anything. How could anyone explain to someone in such a society the concept of light and dark, shades of gray, colors, or the fantastic visual complexity and beauty of nature and the universe? It would be totally impossible. There would be no frame of reference for the person without eyes. It would be just words with no meaning. There would be a dimension of life and experience that such a person could not imagine. Such is the condition of a person who doesn't know God through His Son Jesus Christ. They walk in spiritual darkness and don't know it because they have never experienced spiritual light. This analogy is used in the Word of God many times. Here are some typical examples:

> I was blind, now I see. (John 9:25)

> [I]f our gospel is veiled, it is veiled to those who are perishing, in whose case the god of this world has blinded the minds of the unbelieving so that they might not see the light of the gospel of the glory of Christ, who is the image of God. (II Corinthians 4:3–4)

[Y]ou were formerly darkness, but now you are Light in the Lord. (Ephesians 5:8)

How do you develop the correct belief system about God? To begin with, on the human level, it is impossible. The natural human heart (mind, emotions, will) is born in a state of spiritual darkness that is incapable, by itself, of forming the correct concept or knowledge of God. Actually, this is one of the best evidences of the reality of knowing God. When one experiences the knowledge and love of God for the first time, a very common realization is that it is so different from how humans think and so much more wonderful than ever could have been imagined. A very common type of expression is, "I never could have dreamed that knowing God was like this." It is knowledge and love that is transcendent. Knowing God is above, beyond, deeper, and more profound than anything in natural human imagination or experience. It is eternal and spiritual. Something springs up inside one's being that is like coming back to life from the dead. All of life takes on a different perspective. Nature is more beautiful, relationships are more wonderful, and life becomes more real and satisfying with a purpose and direction. Best of all, a passion and love for God fills one's being with "joy inexpressible and full of glory" (I Peter 1:8).

If it is impossible, then how can you come to the correct belief system and come to know and love God? God Himself must show the way. The Bible teaches that no one can come to God or receive anything from Him unless God Himself initiates the process. Jesus said, "No one can come to Me, unless the Father who sent me draws him" (John 6:44). All through the Bible, from Genesis to Revelation, is a consistent record of God reaching out to man. God communicates with man directly, through nature, circumstances, conscience, dreams, and visions, but most of the time through His Word, the Bible. If a person wants to draw near to God, that desire was first given by God. That person must respond to the desire on God's terms. It is a great error to conclude that drawing near to God is left up to our

The Wind That Never Changes

imagination or interpretation. He has made very clear how we are to draw near to Him. Only His way will work. Human nature thinks the way to God is by finding out what He wants and trying to please Him. God's wants to reveal to us what He has done for us in Jesus Christ and give us grace to believe and receive His Salvation.

God's way is through His Only Son, Jesus Christ. There is no other way. Jesus said, "I am the way, and the truth, and the life; no one comes to the Father but through me" (John 14:6). Notice, Jesus is *the* way, not *a* way. If we are to come to God, we must come to terms with Jesus Christ, who He is, and what He has done for us. Jesus walked on the earth some 2000 years ago and claimed to be God. That is the primary reason He was killed by crucifixion: He claimed to be God. The people of His day understood perfectly that He claimed to be God and considered Him a blasphemer. They thought they were doing God a favor by killing Jesus. Unto this day, some 2000 years later, Jesus is still controversial. His name makes people uncomfortable. Unless His name is used as a curse word or oath, most people do not want to talk about Jesus.

Jesus means "Jehovah is Salvation." It was a common name in His day and is a common name today in some cultures. While it is a name that others have used, God has declared that the name *Jesus* is "the name which is above every name" (Philippians 2:9) and that "there is no other name under heaven that has been given among men by which we must be saved" (Acts 4:12). In biblical times, the name of a person often was linked to that person's character and work. Therefore, Christ Jesus is "The Anointed Savior." His name represents who He is and what He has done. He is the I AM (Exodus 3:14) that spoke to Moses in the burning bush. He used this title many times, and his enemies wanted to kill him for using the name I AM (John 8:58). Only God is I AM. Jesus was, is, and ever shall be God.

The deity of the man Jesus Christ of Nazareth, who walked on the earth some two thousand years ago, lived a perfect sinless life, was crucified for the sins of the world, and was bodily raised on the third day alive forever, is the foundation of Christianity. Jesus claimed and showed Himself to be God. He publicly forgave sins many times. His enemies correctly pointed out that only God can forgive sins. He said, "I am the Son of God" (John 10:36). We are not given the option to consider Jesus as just a prophet, great teacher, good example, etc. He is all these things, but He said and demonstrated by His actions that He is God. No other religious leader claimed to be Almighty God, the I AM. All through the first four books of the New Testament, Jesus made this claim consistently by His actions and words. The only correct worldview for a true Christian is *Jesus Christ*.

Righteousness

Jesus Christ of Nazareth is absolutely central to God's plan of salvation for the human race. *The cross is God's Masterpiece.* God's plan of salvation is so far above human ability it cannot be comprehended or described. It is beyond understanding. If this seems hard to grasp, consider a baby that is less than two months old. The baby knows his mother, but the baby cannot understand his mother or comprehend the mother in an intellectual manner. The relationship between the baby and mother is not based on understanding from the baby's point of view. Yet the relationship works just fine. It works because it is based on love. The baby knows his mother's love and care. This is the way with true Christianity. We can never comprehend God or have an intellectual relationship with Him based on our limited level of understanding. We can, like the young baby, know and enjoy His love. A relationship between God and a human being is primarily one of the heart, not the intellect. The emotions, intellect, and will participate, yet as stated before, they are necessary but not sufficient.

Jesus Christ is essential for God's salvation because of God's definition of righteousness. Most people have some idea of the concept of righteousness or "being good." But how good is good enough for God? There are many answers to this question depending on the person being asked. However, only God's answer counts! What does God have to say about being good enough? He has told us in His Word that His standard of being righteous or good enough is absolute moral perfection: "For whoever keeps the whole law and yet stumbles in one point, he has become guilty of all" (James 2:10). Any bad thought or action in a person's life will keep that person out of Heaven. The Bible calls bad actions and thoughts sin. The Bible also says that no sin shall enter God's Holy presence (Revelation 21:27). If we do not like this definition of righteousness, what is our alternative? Unfortunately, most people make up their own standard of being good enough. This is a tragic eternal error: "For not knowing about God's righteousness and seeking to establish their own, they did not subject themselves to the righteousness of God" (Romans 10:3). If God's standard of righteousness is to be as perfect and Holy as He is, how can we ever make it? *That is precisely the point!* On our own, we can't. "It is impossible" (Mark 10:27). Thanks be to God, He has made a Way.

Jesus Christ had to be born of a virgin, because the Bible teaches that the sin nature is inherited from the father. It tells us that Adam, "begat in his own likeness, after his image" (Genesis 5:3). We all inherited from our earthly father a tendency to want our own way. If you do not believe this, consider a young child. A child of two or three does not need to be taught lying or selfishness. It is built into the child's nature. Anyone who has raised children knows this. Parents never need to explain to a two-year-old how to lie and escape responsibility for bad actions. A two-year old's comprehension is not ready for an explanation on why people lie or act selfishly. However, the two-year-old has no problem figuring it out on his own, and surprisingly early. This does not imply that people do only bad things. Sometimes people do good things. No matter how much good a person may do, it will never be enough by God's standard. Indeed, God's comment on the human race is, "There is none righteous, not even one" (Romans 3:10). Not a single person in

Adam's race can be called good because, "There is only One who is good" (Matthew 19:17). The Word of God refers to all human beings as sinners.

The concept of sin may be considered old-fashioned, but the true salvation of God cannot be understood without a discussion of sin. The basis of sin in the human heart is our will. We want our own way. We do not like to humble ourselves, submit to others, or admit we are wrong. We know we are wrong, but we do not want to admit it, even to ourselves. Pride is the greatest wall that people put between themselves and God. "God is opposed to the proud" (James 4:6). If we are holding on to our own prideful, willful, selfish thoughts and emotions in believing we know enough or we don't need God, we will never come to a saving knowledge of Him. The path to God is through humility: "A broken and a contrite heart, O God, You will not despise" (Psalm 51:17). Submission to God is agreeing with His opinion of us that we are indeed rebellious and willful. It is tempting to think that we are not that bad. By whose standard? God's standard is the only standard that counts, and He says we are sinners. Actually, it is a little worse than this. We are sinners by nature, not by actions. I am not a sinner because I sin. I sin because I am a sinner. Remember the little child example earlier. We are willful and alienated from God because our nature is darkened and not spiritually alive. The Word of God says "you were dead in your trespasses and sins" (Ephesians 2:1) before coming to know Jesus Christ. In this darkened state we are incapable of knowing God. We may know about Him, but we cannot know Him. Knowing about Him will not do: "You believe that God is one. You do well; the demons also believe, and shudder" (James 2:19).

So how did God solve this impossible problem? He took on human nature Himself. God the Son has always existed from eternity past. The Word of God teaches that Jesus as second Person of the Godhead was the creator of all things (John 1:3, Hebrews 1:2). God the Son entered the human race born of a human mother, but He did not have a human father. Since He did not have a human father, he was not born spiritually dead like all other humans. Being born spiritually alive, He did not have the sin nature that all human beings have. He never sinned a single time in His entire life. He was perfect in the absolute moral sense. He was the only human that met God's perfect standard of righteousness. He was also the only person who ever kept the Ten Commandments.

The first Commandment is "You shall have no other gods before Me" (Exodus 20:3). The *other gods* include my will and everything that implies. If my will is higher in my heart than God's will, it becomes a god in my heart, and I break the first Commandment. Another way of stating the first Commandment is "You shall love the Lord your God with all your heart and with all your soul and with all your might" (Deuteronomy 6:5). Notice the three *alls*. *All my heart* means nothing else in my heart even comes close to my love for God—not my spouse, children, career, friends, or anything. *All my soul* means my entire life is 100 percent devoted to God all the time. *All my might* means I do this with every last ounce of strength I have. Can anyone actually do this perfectly? *Of course not!* That is because we are all sinners. A sinner is anyone who cannot keep God's law perfectly. *Jesus did.* He loved His Father like the first Commandment says. He is the only One who kept the law of God perfectly as a human being. Therefore, He is the only human being who has ever been good and righteous by God's standard.

"He made Him who knew no sin to be sin on our behalf, so that we might become the righteousness of God in Him" (II Corinthians 5:21). We need to understand this verse clearly, because it is in this verse that the impossible becomes possible. When Jesus was crucified on the cross, He became our sin bearer. That is, He took upon Himself God's wrath against all sin and experienced God's just judgment for sin. God has declared that "the wages of sin is death" (Romans 6:23). Someone has to die for sin. Either we die for our own sin, or we acknowledge a substitute who was willing to die for us. So Jesus was willing to take the judgment for our sins, and God the Father was willing to give Him the punishment that we should get for sin. If we receive the sacrifice that Jesus made for us, we not only escape God's just judgment against us for our sins, but also God is willing to give us as a free gift the righteousness of Jesus. This is the Divine Exchange that happens at the cross. God gave Jesus the punishment for our sins and gives us the perfect righteousness of Jesus. Why would God do this fantastic thing? Because "God so loved the world" (John 3:16).

So then, all we have to do is believe that Jesus is the Son of God, died for our sins, and rose from the grave on the third day, and God gives us the righteousness of Jesus as a "free gift" (Romans 6:23). Well, not quite. A lot of people believe these very things, yet they do not know Jesus personally. The problem comes from what the word *believe* means from God's viewpoint.

Faith

> And without faith it is impossible to please Him, for he who comes to God must believe that He is and that He is a rewarder of those who seek Him. (Hebrews 11:6)

Someone said that "faith is just believing what God says He will do." This is true, but we still need to discuss the word *believe* and what it means to have *saving faith* by believing. First of all, faith is a gift from God, because "God has allotted to each a measure of faith" (Romans 12:3). It is the Holy Spirit of God who dwells in the believer that imparts faith to the human heart and "teaches you about all things" (I John 2:27).

To believe can mean many things. One meaning is to "acknowledge a fact." Someone you have never met before could tell you he is a helicopter pilot and show you his pilot's license. You believe him. This is belief that has no cost to you personally. The next day you are at the airport and see the same person. He invites you to go up with him for a helicopter ride. If you go with him, this is belief that requires commitment and action. If you do not know how to fly a helicopter, you are putting your life in his hands because of your belief. If you have never seen him fly before, you don't know by observation or experience that he can fly a helicopter. This is belief that is costly. You commit your life to his word and your confidence in his word. So then, faith is believing that produces commitment and action. Another way to think of saving faith is, "believing that leads to trust that leads to action." If there is no trust and commitment, there will be no action and no faith. As the Bible says, "faith, if it has no works, is dead" (James 2:17).

This brings up another important point on faith. The person making the promise must have two things: integrity and the resources to deliver. The helicopter pilot must be telling the truth and have a properly-maintained helicopter. Suppose someone promises to give you a large amount of money in one week. If you know the person is honest and has the ability to give away such an amount of money, you get excited. You don't actually have the money yet, but you are confident the money will come, because "He who promised is faithful" (Hebrews 10:23). You start thinking and acting like you have the money even though you don't have a penny yet. This is faith, and the action is "joy and peace in believing" (Romans 15:13). Your confidence in the one who promised is such that you see the money as yours already, *based on the promise alone.* Sure enough, in one week the money is delivered as promised, and faith becomes sight.

> God is not a man, that He should lie, Nor a son of man, that he should repent; Has He said, and will He not do it? Or has He spoken, and will He not make it good? (Numbers 23:19)

The final point to discuss on faith is attitude. We must acknowledge our state and need before faith will work. A drowning person does not need a lecture on why he needs a life preserver, but in general, most people do not realize their true spiritual state. Sometimes it comes after great trauma or tragedy in life. A serious illness, loss of a loved one, financial loss, and similar situations often are necessary for us to learn that we are weak and needy. God simply wants us to acknowledge our true need before Him, that we are sinners who cannot save ourselves. As long as we feel that we can make it on our own, or we do not think we are so bad, we will not be capable of receiving saving faith from God. *The human heart can have only one master.* God will not compete with our will. He requires that He be Lord or Master of our lives. If we insist on being master of our lives, we prevent His grace from reaching us, drawing us to Him, and healing our hearts.

The required attitude is absolute surrender with no secret agenda. Let's go back to the helicopter ride. You decide to go for a ride and get in the helicopter. You tell the pilot you will go for a ride, but insist on one condition: you must keep one of your feet on the ground. While this is absurd, it illustrates the key reason most people do not come to know the Lord Jesus Christ: They choose conditional commitment. This is why the drowning man analogy is so appropriate. Someone who is drowning is not going to argue about some trivial detail like the color of the life preserver. He just wants to be saved by any means possible. He also knows that he is out of all options. Nothing else is left. He is going to drown if help does not come. *This is exactly the attitude God requires when we come to Him: no options, no arguments.* This is a difficult place to reach if everything seems to be going well. If we are willing, however, the Holy Spirit of God can reveal to us our darkened, lost state without Christ. Like the drowning man, we are willing to admit that we are morally bankrupt and call on a merciful and gracious God to save us. This attitude is also known as repentance. We agree with God that we are sinners by nature and action, and our desire is to turn from our own way and turn to Him with our whole heart. Then He can save us and give us a new nature that does not enjoy any form of sin. Remember, sin before God includes thoughts of pride, jealousy, criticism, an unforgiving attitude, unbelief regarding the things of God, and even fear. It is not just the gross stuff that we normally think of as sin.

There is a bumper sticker that says, "God is my Copilot."

While this is a nice thought, it is not what God really requires. Let's say you are driving your car down the road of life. Your car is your life, and you are in the driver's seat. As you go along the road, you see someone ahead flagging you down. You stop and realize it is Jesus. He says, "I want to go with you." You say, "Great Lord; hop in the back seat." He says "No." You reply, "OK, hop in the front seat and ride shotgun." Jesus says, "I will go with you only if I can drive." Many people want God in their lives, but they do not want to surrender their lives to Him completely. Then when things don't go so well, they run to God to fix the mess they have made. That is why He insists on driving. He knows we don't really know how to live our lives. The problem is, we think we do. When we let Him take over the driver's seat, we are agreeing with Him that we want more than His help. We want Him to take over. True Christians are criticized that they want God as a crutch. True Christians don't want God as a crutch. They want Him to be their intensive care unit. The fact is, God is everyone's intensive care unit, because "He Himself gives to all people life and breath and all things" (Acts 17:25) and "in Him we live and move and exist" (Acts 17:28). Until we really know Him, we do not realize this.

Receiving Him

But as many as received Him, to them gave He the right to become children of God, even to those who believe in His name, who were born, not of blood, nor of the will the flesh nor of the will of man, but of God. (John 1:12–13)

There are two kinds of people in the world: those who know Jesus and those who do not; those who are in Christ and those who are not; those who have the Spirit of Jesus in them and those who do not; those who have been born again by the Spirit of God and those who have not; those who have Jesus in their hearts and those who do not; those who have called upon His name and those who have not; those who have confessed Him as Lord and those who have not. All these statements are biblical expressions of the same thing. It is in or out, with nothing in the middle. The Bible teaches that salvation is like being "born again" (John 3:3). It requires a definite event that is profound and changes us forever, like being born physically. Like physical birth, it takes us from one experience of life into another. Now we will discuss how to take that step of faith and soar with God on "wings like eagles" (Isaiah 40:31).

> God has given us eternal life, and this life is in His Son. He who has the Son has the life; he who does not have the Son of God does not have the life. (I John 5:11–12)

There it is. It is this simple. If we have Jesus, we have eternal life. If we do not, we don't. Now, how do we get Him? Or rather, how does He get us?

> Behold, I stand at the door and knock; if any one hears My voice and opens the door, I will come in to him. (Revelation 3:20)

In this verse Jesus is speaking. He is asking you to let Him come into your heart and life. It is your choice. The door is the door to your heart. Only you can open the door. He will not open it for you. You must open the door and invite Him into your heart and life. *If you open the door, He promises to come in to you.* How do you know this? He cannot lie. He is bound by His Holy Word, which "cannot be broken" (John 10:35). If you open the door, He will come in. If you open the door of your heart and invite Jesus to come in and take over your life, you have taken that definite step and are born again by the Holy Spirit of God.

Many years ago I was talking to a young girl about knowing Jesus as her Savior. I asked her if she had ever asked Jesus to come into her heart. She said, "Yes, every night." I realized that her prayer was not said in faith. I explained to her that when we ask Jesus to come into our hearts, we only need to ask once and believe that He did come into our hearts, just as He promised. Her face lit up with the understanding. All she had to do was ask once and believe that He came in. We prayed, and she asked Jesus into her heart. After she prayed, I asked her where Jesus is. She said, "In my heart." I said, "How do you know?" She said,

The Wind That Never Changes

"Because He promised to come in." That conversation took place over forty years ago. Since then I have observed many people take the same step she took: "repentance towards God and faith in our Lord Jesus Christ" (Acts 20:21).

It is not uncommon at this point for a battle of sorts to be going on in your heart. Something in you wants to believe this, but you are not sure. Your thoughts may be filled with "what ifs." What if God wants me to do something I don't want to do? What if I have to give up something that I really enjoy? What if I turn into a religious fanatic? What if none of this is true or valid at all? Or, what about the people that have never heard about Jesus? What about all the other world religions that don't believe in Jesus? Why, if God is so loving and powerful, does He allow so much pain and suffering? What will my family and friends think? Born again Christians are so hypocritical anyway. I would not like to become like them. The Word of God says, "Each one of us will give an account of himself to God" (Romans 14:12). He will not ask us about our opinions of others. We will have to give an account of how we alone responded to His love. He will not be interested in our arguments about either the people in other cultures that we thought never had a chance to know God or Christians in our life that we considered hypocritical. We will all stand before Him for judgment of our life and our life alone.

Considering these above "what ifs" and "what abouts," are they not to some degree cover-ups for the real issue? *We do not want to give up control of our own lives, even to God!* It is part of human nature to want control. It is time for real honesty. Something in your heart you may not understand is telling you that what you have read in this essay is true. You know it, but you may be afraid to believe it or act on it. If you sense any desire in your heart to respond to Jesus Christ in brokenness and humility and give Him your life, this desire can only come from God the Holy Spirit. No human heart can come to this place without God. It is decision time. You alone can decide. It is tragic beyond comprehension to allow something like our own limited knowledge and understanding to keep us from "so great a salvation" (Hebrews 2:3).

If you have decided to take that eternal step to salvation in Jesus Christ, here is a suggested prayer for you to pray to God. It is best if you pray it out loud because "with the mouth confession is made unto salvation" (Romans 10:10, KJV). It is a suggested prayer, but it is your prayer. This is between you and God.

> Lord Jesus, I come to You as a sinner. I cannot save myself. Without You, I am lost and helpless. I want to turn from my willful life and anything in my life that does not please You. Thank You for dying on the cross for me personally and taking the punishment for my sin. Lord Jesus, I ask you right now to come into my heart and be my Savior and Lord. I open the door of my heart and let You come in and take over my life completely. From this day forth, "for me to live is Christ" (Philippians 1:21, KJV). Thank You Lord Jesus for coming into my heart and taking over my life. Thank You for taking away all my sin and giving me Your righteousness. Thank You Lord Jesus that God is now my Father, and I am his true child. Amen.

If you prayed this prayer seriously and sincerely from your heart, then you are now a true Christian. Now you know that you "have the life" because you "have the Son" (I John 5:11–12). How do you know? You answer that question. From now on, it is you and God.

What about feelings? Sometimes, when a person comes to Jesus, a rush of deep emotional joy occurs. But sometimes it does not. It depends on whether God is pleased to give pleasant feelings at that time. God will surely confirm His ownership of you after you have given your life to Him. It may be instantly or take a little time. Learn from the beginning to walk by faith and not feelings. As time goes on in our walk with God, it does not matter whether we were one of those people who had great feelings the moment we received the Lord Jesus into our hearts or we felt no particular emotion. The important thing is to learn to live by faith. We know we belong to God through faith in His Son because of His promises in His Holy Word, the Bible. Consider an old-fashioned train that has only three cars: a steam locomotive, coal tender, and caboose. The power to pull the train is generated in the steam locomotive when it is fueled by the coal from the coal tender. The caboose is pulled along for the ride, contributing nothing to the movement of the train. Let these three train cars, the steam locomotive, coal tender, and caboose, be called fact, faith, and feelings. The power is in the fact, the Word of God that "cannot be broken" (John 10:35). Faith is like the coal in the tender that fuels the fact. When we believe God, it releases His power in our hearts and lives. So faith releases fact by believing what God says in His Word. Feelings come along afterward.

If our order is correct—fact is first, faith in the fact second—then feelings are in the right place. All too often, feelings are put at the head of the train. There is no power in feelings. If we trust or take seriously our feelings in our relationship to God, there will be days that we wonder if there is a God. His way is for us to focus on His "precious and magnificent promises" (II Peter 1:4). When we do this, the right feelings will surely follow. Our relationship to God cannot be based on something as variable and vulnerable as human emotion. Holy emotions are wonderful to experience, but we are not saved or kept by holy emotions. We are saved and kept by the "power of God" (I Corninthians 2:5), which cannot be shaken. Everything else can and will be shaken.

Eternal Life

Before we come to the knowledge of God the Father through repentance and faith in His Son the Lord Jesus Christ, we have one nature in our hearts. This nature is characterized by self-sufficiency, pride, and seeking its own things. When Jesus comes into our hearts, we have a new nature. It is characterized by total dependence on God, humility, and seeking the things of God and others before our own things. After we are born again, we have two natures. Before God's salvation we had only one choice, that being what our darkened, spiritually-dead heart wanted. After Jesus comes into our heart we have a choice for the first time in our life. We can choose God's will or our own will. The conflict between our old nature and our new nature in Jesus will rage the rest of our physical lives. The power to want and choose God's will comes from the Holy Spirit, who was given to live in us when we received Jesus.

The old nature is called many things in the Bible: the flesh, the old man, the carnal nature, the natural man. Prior to coming to Jesus we lived our life in the power of the old nature. Overcoming the influence of the old nature in our lives will not come instantly. We are full of memories, habits, and attitudes that are typical of the old nature. Sanctification is the process of putting the old nature and its ways to death. This happens by habitually denying what it wants in our hearts and choosing the new nature and what it wants. An old believer put it this way: "There are two dogs fighting in my heart. One is bad; the other is good. The one that wins is the one I feed." We feed the old nature by disobeying God, and we feed the new nature by obeying God. We feed the new nature by reading, studying, memorizing, and meditating on God's Holy Word, the Bible. We also feed the new nature by personal prayer and fellowship with other believers in a sound Church that puts the Lord Jesus where the Bible puts Him:

> He is the image of the invisible God, the firstborn of all creation ... so that He Himself will come to have first place in everything. (Colossians 1:15–18)

> And He is the radiance of His [the Father's] glory and the exact representation of His [the Father's] nature, and upholds all things by the word of His power. When He had made purification of sins, He sat down at the right hand of the Majesty on high. (Hebrews 1:3)

As a Christian we have three great enemies; they are the world, our old nature, and the devil. Yes, there is a literal devil and his demonic kingdom. This is something that is discovered when we get our "spiritual eyes." We do not have to be afraid of him with Jesus in our heart, "because greater is He who is

The Wind That Never Changes

in you than he who is in the world" (I John 4:4). The world is all the people who do not know Jesus as Lord and Savior. Unfortunately, this includes the vast majority of the people that are alive at any time on the earth because "there are few who find" (Matthew 7:14) eternal life in Jesus. As we have discussed, an unsaved person does not know that he is walking in spiritual darkness. He also does not know that he is under the devil's power by default. Until we surrender our life in repentance and faith to Jesus, we are under the power and influence of the devil's kingdom. This kingdom includes all the people in the world who do not know Jesus. "We know that we are of God, and that the whole world lies in the power of the evil one" (I John 5:19). This is the reason there is so much death and suffering in human history. As a nonbeliever we were God's enemy and the devil's pawn. As believers in Jesus, we are God's friend but the devil's spiritual enemy. Before we came to Jesus we could do no harm to the devil's kingdom and in fact, we unintentionally helped in his kingdom. Now we can do great harm to the devil's kingdom because we know and have the Truth.

The devil's first priority is to "blind the minds of the unbelieving so that they might not see the light of the gospel of the glory of Christ, who is the image of God" (II Corinthians 4:3–4). If he fails at this, his next priority is to make believers in Jesus weak and ineffective. To accomplish this task, he uses the world of unbelievers and the value system that he has deceived them into believing. The devil's value system is designed "to steal and kill and destroy" (John 10:10). He plays on all the weaknesses and failures of fallen human nature without Christ: greed, power, lust, pride, anger, fear, criticism, selfishness, self-sufficiency, self-pity, materialism, self-gratification, and the like. The devil knows that such things will not bring joy or fulfillment but destruction and death. As unbelievers, we all bought into the lies of the devil to varying degrees. As believers in Jesus, however, our response is to "Submit therefore to God. Resist the devil and he will flee from you" (James 4:7). We are bombarded with the ungodly value system of the world every day of our lives. As believers we must not allow the value system of the world to choke us spiritually so that we become unfruitful. "Therefore be careful how you walk, not as unwise but as wise, making the most of your time, because the days are evil" (Ephesians 5:15–16).

At a high school commencement program, a speaker made a comment regarding sending our children out into the world: "Ships are safe in harbors, but that's not what ships are for." Like the young people graduating that day, we have launched out into the vast ocean of life. There are beautiful days, stormy days, days we cannot see the sun, rainy days, foggy days, times of darkness, and times of light. We sail along and are subject to the many winds that fill the sails of our heart. Some winds are better than others. Some winds blow us and seek to sink or wreck the ship of our lives. With the Lord Jesus as our Captain, we can be sure that we will arrive at our destination safely. "Jesus Christ is no security against storms, but He is perfect security in storms. He has never promised you an easy passage, only a safe landing" (3). His Spirit fills the sails of our heart with "The Wind that never changes."

NOTES

1. Blaise Pascal, *Pensées*.

2. Bernard of Clairvaux, "Jesus, the Very Thought of Thee," trans. Edward Caswall (1849).

3. L. B. E. Cowman, *Streams in the Desert*, (Zondervan, 2008).

ESSAY II

Doctrine of Baptism

Introduction

The purpose of this essay is to present a biblical discussion of Christian baptism that includes what it is, why it is important, and how it is to be practiced in the church. Specifically, the main goal is to discuss what is meant by the phrase *one baptism* in Ephesians 4:5. Prayerful study and meditation on the referenced passages in this essay will allow a more accurate understanding of common questions on baptism. Why is water baptism important? Is water baptism essential for salvation? Who should be baptized and when, infant or adult? Should sprinkling or immersion be used for baptism? What does baptism really mean or symbolize?

> But when He, the Spirit of truth, comes, He will guide you into all the truth. (John 16:13a)

To understand the doctrine of baptism is to study the process of God's salvation. A person does not have to understand the process of procreation to be a human being. Similarly, a Christian does not have to understand the process of salvation to be a real Christian. However, God gives us information on the process of salvation in His Word and it really helps to have some understanding of this process when it comes to successfully living the Christian life. Simply put, the successful Christian life is one in which "righteousness, peace, and joy" (Romans 14:17) are the rule in daily living and not the exception. These three attributes are independent of human ability and circumstances. Their Source is the life of Christ Himself inhabiting the believer (Romans 5:10). Thus, the ultimate goal and expression of the Christian life is "Christ in you, the hope of glory" (Colossians 1:27).

The doctrine of baptism explains how Christ can literally inhabit the life of a human being in reality. There is mystery in this doctrine (I Corninthians 2:7). Similar to procreation, the process is not completely understood. For example, microbiology has not discovered the source of all the information necessary for the various types of cells in the embryo to differentiate and form complex different structures like the eye or brain. It is not in the DNA. The information in the DNA is to produce all the different types of proteins to build the complex structures in the body. The location of the information in the cell to direct the formation of the complex structures themselves has not been fully understood. It is obviously there, but where it is and how it works is not completely known by science. The point is that we do not have to fully understand the process of procreation to function as a human being. However, some understanding is very helpful in developing modern medicine to help us live better and longer.

God wants us to fully enjoy and experience the benefits of being His children through faith in His Holy Son, the Lord Jesus Christ (John 10:10). He has given us His Holy Word, and in it He has provided all the information we need to live a victorious life for His glory (II Peter 1:2–4). If we do not avail ourselves of this divine information we miss out on the fullness of what it means to be a child of God. Knowing His Word is so important and fundamental to victorious Christian living He has commanded His children to meditate on His Word day and night (Joshua 1:8; Psalm 1:2). The importance of the Word of God in the life of the believer cannot be overstated. In the study of the doctrine of baptism there will be many references to scripture. It is very important for the reader to prayerfully read and meditate on these scriptures, noting the context of each reference. Ultimately, the Holy Spirit is the believer's Teacher (John 14:26; I John 2:27). He is the only One Who can bring revelation to the human heart regarding salvation in Jesus Christ (Galatians 1:12). Understanding the things of God is more than knowledge; it requires revelation from God Himself (Ephesians 3:3).

One Baptism

Like many doctrines in the Word of God, understanding the doctrine of baptism begins with a key verse or verses that are like the linchpins of the doctrine. The linchpin is what holds or brings everything together. The first linchpin reference is, "But I have a baptism to undergo, and how distressed I am until it is accomplished! (Luke 12:50). Note that Jesus made this statement about His undergoing a future baptism that has not yet happened, and He is distressed until this future baptism is finished. This word *distressed* is sometimes translated as *suffering*, *afflicted*, or *pressed*. Jesus has already been baptized by John the Baptist (Matthew 3:13–17). There is no reference anywhere in scripture that He underwent another baptism in water. The key question is what future baptism is He referring to in this verse? That is the question that must be addressed.

The second linchpin reference is Mark 10:35–39:

> James and John, the two sons of Zebedee, came up to Jesus, saying, "Teacher, we want You to do for us whatever we ask of You." And He said to them, "What do you want Me to do for you? They said to Him, "Grant that we may sit, one on Your right and one on Your left, in Your glory." But Jesus said to them, "You do not know what you are asking. Are you able to drink the cup that I drink, or to be baptized with the baptism with which I am baptized?" They said to Him, "We are able." And Jesus said to them, "The cup that I drink you shall drink; and you shall be baptized with the baptism with which I am baptized."

In this second key passage Jesus brings up a future cup He is going to drink and a future baptism that he is going to experience. When the disciples answer they are also able to drink the future cup and experience a future baptism, Jesus does not contradict them but specifically confirms that they both shall indeed drink His cup and shall be baptized with His baptism. The most significant future cup that Jesus will drink is His passion, in which He is rejected by His own people, is abused and tortured by the Romans, takes on the sins of the world, and is killed by crucifixion. This is the cup He asks His Father to let pass from Him (Matthew 26:39). The question is, why would He say that James and John would drink the same cup at some

The Wind That Never Changes

future time? There is no reference of James and John being baptized in water after the resurrection of Jesus. What future baptism for them is Jesus referring to?

There are two arguments that could be made. The future cup is at the Last Supper where Jesus and His disciples eat the Passover and He institutes the Communion meal. A future baptism could be that the disciples were baptized after Pentecost when Peter preached in Acts chapter 2. There is no record in the book of Acts of any of the apostles being baptized except Paul, after he met Jesus on the road to Damascus (Acts 9:18). If the other eleven apostles were baptized in water after the resurrection it is not recorded in scripture. A much better understanding of the future cup emerges after the future baptism is understood. The future cup and future baptism are connected.

When asked for a sign, Jesus gives this reply:

> But He answered and said to them, "An evil and adulterous generation craves for a sign; and *yet* no sign will be given to it but the sign of Jonah the prophet; for just as *Jonah was three days and three nights in the belly of the sea monster* [emphasis added], so will the Son of Man be three days and three nights in the heart of the earth. (Matthew 12:39–40)

Jesus likens His death, burial, and resurrection to the sign of the prophet Jonah. In the book of Jonah, we find this verse: "For You had cast me into the deep, Into the heart of the seas, And the current engulfed me. All Your breakers and billows passed over me (Jonah 2:3). Notice the phrase, "All your breakers and billows passed over me." In Jonah's case all that was happening to him was a result of his disobedience to God and God's judgment upon him by making him suffer in the belly of a great fish. Remember that Jesus said His sign would be similar to the sign of Jonah. Jonah was buried by water over him entering into the depths of God's just judgment upon him. It could have been a watery grave but when Jonah repented and called upon God he was saved (Jonah 2:9–10). It is a picture of death, burial, and resurrection through water.

Psalm 42 is one of many messianic psalms in which we have a prophetic glimpse into the thoughts of Jesus as he was going through His suffering. Psalm 22 and 69 are two other well-known messianic psalms. Jesus quotes the first verse of Psalm 22 on the cross (Matthew 27:46). If people had been paying attention they would have known He was telling them at that very moment what was happening to Him and how He was feeling. In Psalm 42 the Spirit of Jesus reveals to one of the sons of Korah (a Levitical Priest) a prophetic glimpse of how Jesus would feel during His lifetime on earth, and specifically how He would feel during His passion: "Deep calls to deep at the sound of Your waterfalls; All Your breakers and Your waves have rolled over me" (Psalm 42:7). In this verse, the Son of God is prophetically speaking through the writer regarding events that are still 1000 years in the future. Notice how similar this verse is to what Jonah says in the belly of the great fish, particularly "All your breakers and billows passed over me." They are virtually identical.

This is the future baptism that Jesus was talking about in both of the earlier key references. The baptism of the judgment of God upon Him for our sins. Jonah suffered punishment for his own disobedience to God. Jesus suffered the wrath of God for the sins of the world. It was a baptism of judgment in which He, similar to Jonah, went under the waters of Judgment and the waves and breakers of God's wrath broke over Him. Isaiah says it this way:

> [B]y oppression and judgment He was taken away; And as for His generation, who considered That He was cut off out of the land of the living for the transgression of my people, to whom the stroke was due? His grave was assigned with wicked men, Yet He was with a rich man in His death, Because He had done no violence, Nor was there any deceit in His mouth. But the LORD was pleased to crush Him, putting Him to grief; If He would render Himself as a guilt offering, He will see His offspring, He will prolong His days, And the good pleasure of the LORD will prosper in His hand. (Isaiah 53:8–10)

A really amazing truth is that God the Father was pleased to crush God the Son and put Him to grief. Yet, the end of the story is that the Son will see His offspring, because of the price

He paid with His own blood. Here the mystery starts to become apparent. How could God Crush God? Jesus did say of His life "No one has taken it away from Me, but I lay it down on My own initiative. I have authority to lay it down, and I have authority to take it up again. This commandment I received from My Father" (John 10:18). So somehow God the Father poured out His wrath for sin on God the Son, yet the Son had authority to lay down His own life and take it up again. Just like procreation and a lot of other things, we don't have to understand it perfectly to believe and enjoy the benefits of believing

In the Garden on the night Jesus was betrayed, He prayed, "My Father, if it is possible, let this cup pass from Me; yet not as I will, but as You will" (Matthew 26:39). It is clear that Jesus was speaking of the impending events that were about to commence and end with His death by crucifixion. However, the part that He dreaded most was that fateful moment when all the sins of the world would be put on Him and He would become sin and experience the wrath of God in judgment for that sin. He [the Father] made Him [the Son] who knew no sin to be sin on our behalf, so that we might become the righteousness of God [the Father] in Him [the Son] (II Corinthians 5:21). This was the moment on the cross when Jesus cried out, "My God, my God, why have You forsaken me?" (Matthew 27:46). For the first time in eternity the Father and Son were separated because of Jesus being willing to identify with our sin and bear the wrath of God on our behalf. Because of the obedience and sacrifice of Jesus on the cross, we do not have to ever experience separation from God if we are willing to receive what Jesus did on the cross to pay our sin debt and surrender complete control of our life to Him by faith. He drank to the dregs the cup of the wrath of God for sin so we do not have to:

> Thus says your Lord, the LORD, even your God Who contends for His people, "Behold, I have taken out of your hand the cup of reeling, the chalice of My anger; You will never drink it again." (Isaiah 51:22)

If the cup that Jesus said He would drink was the cup of the wrath of God for sin which resulted in His separation from His Father and His death, and the baptism that He was to be baptized with was His death, burial, and resurrection in taking our punishment for sin, how do James and John drink the same cup and become baptized with the same baptism?

> But as many as *received* Him, to them He gave the *right* to become children of God, even to those who *believe* in *His name*, who were *born*, not of blood nor of the will of the flesh nor of the will of man, but of God. (John 1:12-13; emphasis added)

In these two verses from the Gospel of John there are profound truths that are not obvious. Several words have been italicized. It is necessary to go a little deeper into the meaning of these words. English translations of the original Hebrew and Greek of the Bible often do not always convey the depth of what the Author is really saying.

Received is a Greek word that means to take into one's possession and not just passively accept. It is an active word that means a definite action or attitude. If a person is offered something they really want, it is not theirs until they take it. The offered gift is held out and could be offered for a long time. Until an active effort of taking happens, the offered gift is not possessed by the recipient. The salvation offered by Jesus by virtue of His sacrificial death on the Cross is offered to whosoever (Romans 10:13). Only those who take it by faith possess it.

Right in this verse is a word that is used 103 times in the New Testament. In the New American Standard Bible, 69 of those times it is translated *power* and 29 of those times it is translated *authority*. In only two times is it translated *right*. The remaining three are *liberty*, *jurisdiction*, and *strength*. Therefore, it is appropriate to say that God grants a type of power or authority to those who have received Jesus by faith. It seems that *power* may be the most appropriate term. It raises the question, what is this divine power from God intended to accomplish? It will be shown later how this divine power causes the believer in Jesus to drink His cup and be baptized with His baptism.

Believe in English is another word that does not convey the depth of meaning intended by the Author of the Bible. *Believe* in the Greek has the requirement of complete trust or commitment. Think of it as belief that is costly. When a person boards a commercial jet to take a trip they have committed their life to the belief that the airline will safely take them to their destination. While a passenger on that airplane, they have no control whatsoever over their wellbeing or safety. Even if they have a commercial pilot's license and are certified to fly that particular aircraft, how do they know it was properly maintained and prepared for the flight? They don't. Flying on a commercial airplane is a pure act of costly faith. This is what it means to believe in Jesus. He has complete control and ownership of the life of the believer.

His name is the name Jesus.

> And there is salvation in no one else; for there is no other name under heaven that has been given among men by which we must be saved. (Acts 4:12)

> For this reason also, God highly exalted Him, and bestowed on Him the name which is above every name, so that at the name of Jesus *every knee will bow*, of those who are in heaven and on earth and under the earth. (Philippians 2:9–10; emphasis added)

> These things I have written to you who believe in the name of the Son of God, so that you may know that you have eternal life. (I John 5:13)

A careful study of the New Testament will show that the consistent emphasis is always on the name of Jesus. The power for salvation is in the name of Jesus (Acts 4:12). Jesus means "Jehovah is Salvation." His name reveals His character and His work. Salvation is not about what we can do for God, but about believing and receiving what He has done for us in Jesus Christ. The importance of the name of Jesus as it relates to baptism will be shown later.

Born in this verse means *begotten*. *Begotten* is not a word commonly used today. Its meaning carries the clear fact that the one begotten derives its new life from the One doing the begetting. This sounds a little awkward but consider procreation that was discussed earlier. In this human activity, the child receives its life from the mother and father. It is born or begotten of the mother and father. Its life is their life expressed in a new person. Notice again, "who were *born*, not of blood nor of the will of the flesh nor of the will of man, but of God" (John 1:13; emphasis added). The Holy Spirit makes it very clear that the new life that results from receiving Jesus by believing on His name does not come by any human agency! It is impossible for a human being to make this new birth happen. It takes the power of God! Similar to human procreation, the new life in the child of God comes from God Himself. When a person becomes a real Christian, they receive a completely new life from God that they have never possessed before. One meaning of procreate is "to bring into existence." Here again is mystery. In the process of God's salvation in Jesus, He somehow creates a completely new life in the believer. Now a new question arises: If the believer has a completely new life sourced from the life of God Himself, what happened to the old life?

> I have been crucified with Christ; and it is no longer I who live, but Christ lives in me; and the life which I now live in the flesh I live by faith in the Son of God, who loved me and gave Himself up for me. (Galatians 2:20)

A profound and deep mystery is introduced in this verse. Paul the apostle states that he has been crucified with Christ and that he no longer lives. It is interesting to note that Paul does not say "I have died with Christ." He uses the word *crucified*. It is the same Greek word used to describe how the two thieves died on either side of Christ and at the same time (Matthew 27:38). The Greek word means, "crucified with." Paul is saying, "I went through the crucifixion experience with Christ, and not just the last part when He dismissed His spirit." As will be shown later in this essay, Jesus drank the cup on the cross and then dismissed His spirit on the cross. By using the word *crucified*, Paul is saying that he was there with Jesus. This clearly implies that in some mysterious way Paul was with Jesus on the

The Wind That Never Changes

cross and suffered a death.

But, he now has a new life, the very life of Christ Himself. How can this happen? He is still in his fleshly body, but the life force that makes him a living being has dramatically changed. Paul was crucified with Christ and yet Paul lives. This sounds like death, burial, and resurrection—baptism, like Jonah the figure and Jesus the Savior. The clear teaching of New Testament salvation is that it involves the death of the old self and the impartation of the life of Christ Himself into the believer. This happens on the cross. When a person receives Jesus by believing on His name, the Power of God brings about a profound transformation. God literally identifies that person with Christ on the cross, and when Christ dies on the cross that person dies also in the sight of God. The sinful, rebellious nature of man is not to be rehabilitated. God's solution is to put it to death (Romans 8:3).

Taking Paul, the apostle, as an example of all true believers in Jesus, Paul's sins and Paul's sin nature—the old Paul—were laid on Jesus when He was made sin on the cross. Jesus drank the cup of the wrath of God for Paul personally as He did for every believer personally. Jesus completely identified with the sin of Paul and took all the punishment that Paul justly deserved. Paul was identified with Jesus on the cross as all true believers are. In drinking the cup, Jesus paid for all of Paul's sins while He was still alive on the cross. His statement, "It is Finished" (John 19:30) signified the sin debt is paid (Colossians 2:14). Then in the death of Jesus, the old sinful Paul died with Jesus. When Jesus died, Paul died, was buried, and Paul rose from the dead, alive for evermore in Jesus, with the new life of Jesus Himself. This act of spiritual procreation through the death, burial, and resurrection of Jesus Christ is the "one baptism" (Ephesians 4:5) and is carried out by the Holy Spirit: "For by one Spirit we were all baptized into one body, whether Jews or Greeks, whether slaves or free, and we were all made to drink of one Spirit" (I Corinthians 12:13).

In summary, two specific events occurred on the cross. In

both events, every true believer in Jesus Christ is intimately identified. Both are necessary for God's salvation.

First, Jesus took the cup of the wrath of God for our sins, "and He Himself is the propitiation for our sins; and not for ours only, but also for those of the whole world" (I John 2:2). This *propitiation* or "pay the penalty of" our sins reached its culmination on the cross from about noon till 3:00 in the afternoon during the time when there was darkness over the earth (Matthew 27:45). It was during this time that "the LORD was pleased to crush Him, putting Him to grief; If He would render Himself as a guilt offering, He will see His offspring, He will prolong His days, and the good pleasure of the LORD will prosper in His hand" (Isaiah 53:10). The Father turned His face from the Son and the wrath for our sins was laid upon Him:

> At the ninth hour [3:00 in the afternoon] Jesus cried out with a loud voice, "Eloi, Eloi, lama sabachthani?" which is translated, "my God, my God, why have You forsaken Me?" (Mark 15:34)

> Therefore when Jesus had received the sour wine, He said, "It is finished!" And He bowed His head and gave up His spirit. (John 19:30)

"It is finished" was the sixth of the last seven statements Jesus made on the cross before He died. By speaking these words, He signified that the complete payment for all the sins of the world was accomplished. Psalm 22 begins with "My God, my God, why hast thou forsaken me?" and ends with "He hath done it." "He hath done it" is a prophetic "It is finished."

Second, Jesus experienced a baptism through His death, burial, and resurrection, as discussed earlier. Every true believer is united with Jesus in this baptism, which is carried out by the Holy Spirit.

> For if we have become united with Him in the likeness of His death, certainly we shall also be in the likeness of His resurrection, knowing this, that our old self was crucified with Him, in order that our body of sin might be done away with, so that we would no longer be slaves to sin. (Romans 6:5–6)

> Even so consider yourselves to be dead to sin, but alive to God in Christ Jesus. (Romans 6:11)

The Wind That Never Changes

This is the Divine exchange that happens through the cross (II Corinthians 5:21).

There is an interesting and relevant correlation between the Jewish rite of circumcision in the Old Testament and water baptism in the New Testament. It is also interesting that Paul, under inspiration from the Holy Spirit, brings up the subject of spiritual circumcision to the Colossians, who were gentiles:

> See to it that no one takes you captive through philosophy and empty deception, according to the tradition of men, according to the elementary principles of the world, rather than according to Christ. For in *Him* all the fullness of Deity dwells in bodily form, and in *Him* you have been made complete, and *He* is the head over all rule and authority; and in *Him* you were also circumcised with a circumcision made without hands, in the *removal of the body of the flesh* by the circumcision of Christ; *having been buried with Him in baptism*, in which you were also raised up with *Him* through faith in the working of God, who raised *Him* from the dead. When you were dead in your [1.] transgressions and [2.] the uncircumcision of your flesh, He [the Father] made you alive together with *Him* [the Son], having forgiven us all our transgressions, having canceled out the certificate of debt consisting of decrees against us, which was hostile to us; and He [the Father] has taken it out of the way, having nailed it to the cross. (Colossians 2:8–14; emphasis added)

The numbers *1* and *2* are added in brackets in this passage to highlight that there were two problems related to sin taken care of through the cross: 1. transgressions and 2. uncircumcision of our flesh. Jesus drinking the cup of the wrath of God paid for the transgressions. His death, burial, and resurrection circumcises our flesh or, as discussed before, puts the sin nature to death. As the above passage states, "in Him you have been made complete." This completeness in Christ includes complete payment for all sins, death of the old nature, and new resurrection life in Christ. This all is accomplished by Jesus on the cross.

The obvious, central, powerful focus in this passage is Christ —who He is and what He has done. The clear emphasis of salvation is *in* and *with* Him. In and with Him, the believer has been both circumcised and baptized in Christ through faith in the working of God. The Greek word for *working* in verse 12 occurs eight times in the New Testament. It is always used in the context of supernatural power. So it would more accurately read, "though faith in the supernatural power of God." Salvation in Christ through faith is a supernatural act by an infinite, all powerful God. The believer's identity with Christ on the Cross is a mystery that only God understands and accomplishes. That is why Paul, under the inspiration of the Holy Spirit, warns believers not to get led astray by shallow, powerless arguments regarding how we can be just before a Holy God (Colossians 2:16–18).

Shallow and Powerless Theology

Shallow and powerless arguments are very important to consider because modern Christianity is full of such doctrines. Circumcision in the Old Testament is analogous to baptism in the New Testament (Colossians 2:8–14). Both should be an outward sign of an inward, heart reality. However, in both Old Testament physical circumcision and New Testament water baptism, the worshiper's focus is more on the act and not the heart. The Old Testament worshiper concludes, "I have been circumcised; I am in right standing before God." Similarly, the New Testament worshiper says, "I have been water baptized; therefore I am a Christian." As an example, consider a discussion of circumcision in Romans 2:25–29. In this passage the word *baptism* could be used instead of the word circumcision and the word *grace* could be replace *the Law*. In both cases, the meaning and conclusions are the same. If there is not a heart transformation by faith, O. T. physical circumcision and N. T. water baptism are meaningless rituals. Colossians 2:8–14 discussed previously links supernatural circumcision and supernatural baptism to the supernatural working of God. Both physical circumcision and water baptism are symbolic outward acts of a supernatural spiritual transformation in which the death of the old nature occurs.

> For indeed circumcision [baptism] is of value if you practice the Law [grace]; but if you are a transgressor of the Law [grace], your circumcision [baptism] has become uncircumcision [un-baptism]. So if the uncircumcised [un-baptized] man keeps the requirements of the Law [grace], will not his uncircumcision [un-baptism] be regarded as circumcision [baptism]? And he who is physically uncircumcised [un-baptized], if he keeps the Law [grace], will he not judge you who though having the letter of the Law [grace] and circumcision [baptism] are a transgressor of the Law [grace]? *For he is not a Jew [Christian] who is one outwardly, nor is circumcision [baptism] that which is outward in the flesh. But he is a Jew [Christian] who is one inwardly; and circumcision [baptism] is that which is of the heart, by the Spirit, not by the letter; and his praise is not from men, but from God.* (Romans 2:25–28; emphasis added)

In the history of the Old Testament, it did not take long after God gave the Law through Moses for the typical Jewish mentality to develop a shallow and powerless understanding of how they, as God's chosen people, were to relate to Him. The shallow and powerless understanding led to the conclusion that if a male was circumcised and kept the Law of Moses, he was pleasing to God. This concept of ritual and works was not valid in the Old Testament (Isaiah 1:10–17; Psalms 51:16–17) and it is not valid in the New Testament (Ephesians 2:8–9; Titus 3:5).

> If they confess their iniquity and the iniquity of their forefathers, in their unfaithfulness which they committed against Me, and also in their acting with hostility against Me—I also was acting with hostility against them, to bring them into the land of their enemies—or if *their uncircumcised heart* becomes humbled so that they then make amends for their iniquity, then I will remember My covenant with Jacob, and I will remember also My covenant with Isaac, and My covenant with Abraham as well, and I will remember the land. (Leviticus 26:40–42; emphasis added)

Here, in Leviticus, the importance of the heart is emphasized by God. With God, it has always been about the heart. Old Testament salvation is identical to New Testament salvation, which is by grace through faith, as was illustrated in the salvation of Abraham (Genesis 15:6). It has never and will never be due to works. The sin debt is too great (Psalm 49:7-8). It cannot be paid or earned by works. Salvation in both the Old and New

Testaments is about what God has done for us, not about what we could ever do for Him. He calls all our righteous deeds filthy rags (Isaiah 64:6). The wording is different in the Old Testament but the teaching of salvation in Christ is there. Consider what could be called the John 3:16 of the Old Testament.

> Do homage to the Son, that He not become angry, and you perish in the way, For His wrath may soon be kindled. How blessed are all who *take refuge* in Him! (Psalm 2:12; emphasis added)

This verse is talking about Jesus. The Son of God is everywhere in the Old Testament, even as He explained on the Road to Emmaus (John 24:13-35). The translation of the last part of verse 12 is key to seeing why this verse is like John 3:16. Both *take* and *refuge* are the same Hebrew word and they both mean "trust." So a Jew would read the verse, "How blessed are all who *trust, trust* in Him!" In the Hebrew language, when a word is repeated it is to give emphasis. *Trust, trust* to a Jew means to *really trust* for a gentile. So the Holy Spirit is saying to Old Testament sinners in this verse to really trust the promised Messiah that has been promised by God since shortly after Adam and Eve sinned, who will take away our sins (Genesis 3:15). In other words, really trust in God and His promises. The phrase *take refuge* or *trust, trust* occurs thirty-five times in the Old Testament. That is what God always wants: your heart. The good works follow a heart transformation. Good works without a heart surrendered to God are dead works and useless (Hebrews 6:1; 9:14). In the Old Testament it is specifically mentioned in several places that people who did not know God came to know God (I Samuel 3:7; II Chronicles 33:13). It has never been about ritual and works. Both the Old Testament and New Testament saints know God. That is real salvation—to know God.(John 17:3).

The biblical understanding of the *one baptism* in Ephesians 4:5 is the death, burial, and resurrection of Jesus Christ. This is the baptism He was speaking of in Luke 12:50 and in His discussion with James and John in Mark 10:35-39. This is the baptism "through faith in the working of God" by which we are saved.

The Wind That Never Changes

When we, by the grace of God, are enabled by the Holy Spirit (II Timothy 2:25) to humble ourselves in repentance and faith, looking unto Jesus and His sacrifice on the Cross as our only hope for forgiveness and salvation, God reckons these to our account: 1. full payment for all our sins past, present, and future; 2. the death of our old sinful nature with Jesus on the Cross when He dismissed His spirit, and resurrection with Jesus from the tomb to walk in newness of life. These are the cup and the baptism that Jesus said James and John would undergo just as Jesus said He would experience. This same process of salvation applies to every true Christian who really knows Jesus as Savior and Lord. Jesus on the cross paid for the sins of each one of us so personally and identified with our sins so completely, it was as if we were there with him on the cross.

> ...having canceled out the certificate of debt consisting of decrees against us, which was hostile to us; and He has taken it out of the way, having nailed it to the cross. (Colossians 2:14)

The *certificate of debt* for each one of us personally and individually was nailed to the cross in Jesus as He became our sin and took the punishment for our sins. When He died, we died with Him, and when He arose, we arose with Him. This is the clear teaching of scripture as to how we are born again by the supernatural power of God.

The Name Jesus Christ

The main objective of this essay on baptism has been to show what the *one baptism* in Ephesians 4:5 means. This rest of the essay will discuss some of the questions on baptism presented in the first of the essay beginning with whether water baptism is essential for salvation. Some discussion is necessary on scriptures that could be interpreted in a way that teaches water baptism is necessary for salvation. The most often quoted verse is:

> Peter said to them, "Repent, and each of you be baptized *in the name of*

> *Jesus Christ* for the forgiveness of your sins; and you will receive the gift of the Holy Spirit. (Acts 2:38; emphasis added)

Where in this verse is the power for salvation? A careful reading of the rest of the book of Acts and the entire New Testament shows that the power for salvation is the name of Jesus Christ. Similarly, in Paul's conversion and baptism the power is in His name:

> Now why do you delay? Get up and be baptized, and wash away your sins, *calling on His name*. (Acts 22:16; emphasis added)

All though the book of Acts the apostles were persecuted for teaching and taking actions like healing and deliverance in the Name of Jesus. The power of His name is consistently taught and practiced by the apostles:

> ...but these have been written so that you may believe that Jesus is the Christ, the Son of God; and that believing you may have life in *His name*. (John 20:31; emphasis added)

> And it shall be that everyone who calls on *the name of the LORD* will be saved. (Acts 2:21; emphasis added)

> And there is salvation in no one else; for there is *no other name* under heaven that has been given among men by which we must be saved. (Acts 4:12; emphasis added)

> And when they had summoned them, they commanded them not to speak or teach at all *in the name of Jesus*. (Acts 4:18; emphasis added)

> They took his advice; and after calling the apostles in, they flogged them and ordered them not to speak *in the name of Jesus*, and then released them. (Acts 5:40; emphasis added)

> But when they believed Philip preaching the good news about the kingdom of God and *the name of Jesus Christ*, they were being baptized, men and women alike. (Acts 8:12; emphasis added)

> But the Lord said to him, "Go, for he is a chosen instrument of Mine, to *bear My name* before the Gentiles and kings and the sons of Israel." (Acts 9:15; emphasis added)

> Of Him all the prophets bear witness that *through His name* everyone who believes in Him receives forgiveness of sins. (Acts 10:43; emphasis added)

> And he ordered them to be baptized *in the name of Jesus Christ*. Then they

asked him to stay on for a few days. (Acts 10:48; emphasis added)

Whoever will call on *the name of the LORD* will be saved. (Romans 10:13; emphasis added)

... so that at *the name of Jesus* every knee will bow, of those who are in heaven and on earth and under the earth. (Philippians 2:10; emphasis added)

These verses are not presented to suggest that water baptism is not important. It is very important, as will be discussed later. However, careful examination of scripture clearly puts the emphasis on the Name of Jesus for salvation. The error in both Old Testament physical circumcision and New Testament water baptism is exalting what we do over what God has done for us. God has declared that "no flesh shall glory in His Presence" (I Corinthians 1:29). When Jesus said "It is finished" (John 19:30) on the cross, He signified the complete sacrifice for our sins was accomplished.

Good Works

Nothing we could ever do can add to His perfect salvation. Any attempt on our part is just "dead works" (Hebrews 6:1; 9:14). The New Testament teaches that we are not saved by good works of any kind (Ephesians 2:8-9; Titus 3:5). A careful study of the book of James does not contradict the teaching that a person is not saved by works. The letters of Paul and James are written by the same Author, the Holy Spirit.

In Romans chapter 4, Paul is discussing Abraham's initial salvation by grace through faith as recorded in Genesis chapter 15. At this point Abraham is about 85 years old and has been in the land of Canaan for 10 years. Genesis 15:6 reads, "Then he believed in the Lord; and He reckoned it to him as righteousness." This is the moment that Abraham was justified by faith in the sight of God and became an Old Testament believer. This is the point Abraham became rooted in the love and promise of God (Ephesians 3:17). An important and very relevant event immediately follows Abraham's conversion: God and Abraham made a covenant. In the Old Testament, two persons or two groups of persons would make a covenant or agreement (Genesis 15:17; Jeremian 34:18-19). The ceremony would include cutting a calf or other animals into two pieces. The two halves of the severed animal would be placed a small distance apart, leaving enough room to walk between them. Each of the two persons entering into the covenant would walk between the two halves of the animal, signifying they would keep their part of the covenant. In Genesis chapter 15, when God makes a covenant with Abraham, it is important to note that God put Abraham to sleep and only God Himself passed between the two halves of the animals. In this profound act, God is demonstrating to Abraham and to everyone who ever enters into covenant relationship with God by grace through faith, that God holds Himself 100 percent responsible for keeping the covenant. In Romans 4:16 Paul calls Abraham "the father of us all," including both Jewish Old Testament believers and Christian New Testament believers. In Genesis chapter 15 God is demonstrating how all salvation in Him works. *He does it all!* Our role is to believe and by faith receive. Jesus on the cross is a picture of covenant. Instead of being between two animals He was between two criminals. He alone was between them and He alone accomplished something we could never do or earn (Matthew 19:25–26). The covenant maker became the sacrifice. That is why "it is finished" (John 19:30) is such an important statement. We can make no contribution to our salvation. God does it all, just like with the covenant He made with Abraham.

The book of James discusses an event in Abraham's life that occurs approximately twenty-five years after Abraham's salvation by faith and the one-sided covenant God made with him in Genesis chapter 15. In James 2:14–26, James uses an event in Abraham's life when God tested him to illustrate works after salvation. It is important to distinguish works *for* salvation versus works *after* salvation. In Genesis chapter 22 God commands Abraham to offer his son Isaac as a burnt offering on

Mount Moriah. Isaac was the promised heir from God (Genesis 17:19). Abraham's life was bound up in Isaac his son (Genesis 22:2). By this time, Abraham had been walking with God approximately twenty-five years. He was a mature believer. God gave him a very severe trial to test his obedience: kill his own son as a sacrifice to God. By this time in his life Abraham had learned to really trust in God and not question his commands. He obeyed immediately and set off on the three-day journey to Mount Moriah to sacrifice his son as God commanded. Just before Abraham struck Isaac with the knife, God stopped him and showed him a ram in a thicket to sacrifice instead. Abraham's obedience and trust in God's love allowed him to do the unthinkable if God commands it. This is the obedience of a believer that is grounded in the love of God (Ephesians 3:17). Abraham became rooted in the love of God in Genesis 15 and demonstrated that he was grounded in the love of God in Genesis 22. This is the goal of all believers, to not only be rooted but also grounded in the love of God (Ephesians 3:17). The point James is making is summed up in James 2:22, "faith is perfected." Abraham's faith began in Genesis 15:6 and was demonstrated perfected in Genesis 22:10. The growth process took 25 years of walking with God.

Baptism Saves You

> Corresponding to that, baptism now saves you—not the removal of dirt from the flesh, but an appeal to God for a good conscience —through the resurrection of Jesus Christ. (I Peter 3:21)

Many translations put the phrase "not the removal of dirt from the flesh, but an appeal to God for a good conscience" either in parenthesis or set apart by dashes or commas, indicating it is included to give clarity to the reader but does not alter the meaning of the sentence. "Corresponding to that, baptism now saves you through the resurrection of Jesus Christ." This is consistent with the earlier discussion on what baptism really means to the believer, and puts the focus on the death, burial, and resurrection of Jesus Christ rather than a ritual performed by the believer. The writer of Hebrews further gives light on the subject of ritualistic works and the conscience.

> How much more will the blood of Christ, who through the eternal Spirit offered Himself without blemish to God, cleanse your conscience from dead works to serve the living God? (Hebrews 9:14)

In the parenthetic comment, I Peter 3:21 is reminding the believer, consistent with the writer of Hebrews, that a clear conscience does not come from the ritual of baptism or any rituals, but through faith in the resurrection of Jesus Christ. Peter is specifically emphasizing that it is not the act of water baptism that saves us but faith in the working of God through Christ on the cross, which water baptism symbolizes.

Being Born of Water is not Water Baptism

> Jesus answered, "Truly, truly, I say to you, unless one is born of water and the Spirit he cannot enter into the kingdom of God." (John 3:5)

> He saved us, not on the basis of deeds which we have done in righteousness, but according to His mercy, by the washing of regeneration and renewing by the Holy Spirit. (Titus 3:5)

> ...so that He might sanctify her, having cleansed her by the washing of water with the word. (Ephesians 5:26)

> ...for you have *been born again* not of seed which is perishable but imperishable, that is, through the living and enduring word of God. (I Peter 1:23; emphasis added)

> So faith comes from hearing, and hearing by the word of Christ. (Romans 10:17)

The water that Jesus is talking about in John 3:5 is the water of the word of God. Salvation begins with the word of God. A person is born of water (the word of God) when hearing and receiving the word of God leads to repentance and faith in the gospel, which is followed by being baptized by the Holy Spirit and then being baptized in water in obedience to Christ, thus publically proclaiming his identity with the death, burial, and

The Wind That Never Changes

resurrection of Christ (Romans 6:11; Acts 10:44–48).

Water Baptism Is not the Main Thing

> For Christ did not send me to baptize, but to preach the gospel, not in cleverness of speech, so that the cross of Christ would not be made void. (I Corinthians 1:17)

The believers in the Corinthian church were having problems with division. Some were saying, "I am of Paul," and "I of Apollos," and "I of Cephas," and "I of Christ" (I Corinthians 1:12). They seemed to think that who water baptized them was important. Even the true followers of Christ did not have the right attitude. Paul's response is that it is not important who water baptized them. What is most important is the cross of Christ. The gospel message includes water baptism. However, it is not the central focus. The central focus of the gospel is the death, burial, and resurrection of Jesus Christ (I Corinthians 15:1–4).

The goal of this essay is not to diminish the importance of water baptism but rather to exalt the importance of the cross (Galatians 6:14).

Importance of Water Baptism

> Go therefore and make disciples of all the nations, baptizing them in the name of the Father and the Son and the Holy Spirit. (Matthew 28:19)

An ambassador represents the authority, power, and interest of the potentate or government he represents. He does not speak or act on his own authority but on the authority of his sovereign. An ambassador representing a king in a foreign court might address the local authorities with "In the name of the king." That statement from the ambassador has the same authority as if the king himself were present about to declare his desires or decrees. This is true because the king himself told the ambassador what to say or do in his name. If the hearers of the king's ambassador disregard the king's request they must face the authority and power of the king himself. We are ambassadors of Christ (II Corinthians 5:20). As members of His Kingdom we are aliens and strangers in the earthly realm (Hebrews 11:13). The fallen worldly system is ruled by the kingdom of darkness (Luke 4:5-6, John 5:19) and real Christians are members of the kingdom of light (I John 1:5). As such, we should not act casually in the name of Jesus. It is a solemn and serious matter to be His representative in a foreign kingdom.

Jesus the King commanded his ambassadors to baptize in the name of the Father, Son, and Holy Spirit. What is this name? Could it be the name that is above every other name (Philippians 2:9-11)? *Jesus* is the name above every name. In the name of Jesus is embodied the fullness of the Godhead. Jesus is called Eternal Father (Isaiah 9:6). He said, "I and the Father are one" (John 10:30). When we see Jesus we see the Father (John 14:9). Jesus and the Father are one, yet two distinct manifestations of the Godhead. The above scripture passages are given to validate that when we do anything in the name of Jesus, we do it also in the name of the Father. Similarly, Jesus and the Holy Spirit are one. In Romans 8:9-11 all three manifestations of the Godhead are said to indwell the Christian: 1. Spirit of God, 2. Spirit of Christ, and 3. Spirit of Him who raised Jesus from the dead. The three-in-one parts of the Godhead always participate together in salvation. In Romans we see we are 1. justified by faith, 2. justified by blood, 3. justified by grace. In John 14:16-18 Jesus promises to send the Holy Spirit to his disciples. In verse 18 He then says "I will come to you." This clearly shows that where the Holy Spirit is present so is Jesus Himself. This mystery of the three in oneness of the Godhead cannot be understood. There are three manifestations or offices, yet one God. This discussion is presented to suggest that baptizing in the name of Jesus is baptizing in the name of the Father, Son, and Holy Spirit. In the book of Acts, the apostles baptized in the name of Jesus in Acts 2:38, Acts 8:16, Acts 10:48, and Acts 19:5. It may suggest that this was their interpretation as well.

Does it really matter what is said when a believer is baptized? As discussed earlier, what really matters is the heart. The importance of the name of Jesus is realizing that being baptized in His name means coming under His authority, His ownership, His interest, and His Kingdom. We are proclaiming to all that we have forsaken the kingdom of darkness, have received full forgiveness of sins through the merit of His blood, have died with Him on the cross when He died, were buried with Him, and arose with Him with eternal resurrection life. Being water baptized shows that we have repented, believed, received, and submitted to our new King.

Water baptism after heart transformation by the Holy Spirit through faith is the commandment of Jesus. There is no higher authority. The apostles and disciples recognized this fact by the importance they placed on water baptism all through the book of Acts. The modern Christian church does not practice water baptism with the same diligence and consistency as the early Christians. Interestingly, water baptism is practiced more biblically in non-western cultures. In those cultures, the family of a new Christian will not believe their conversion to Christ until they either see or know that they have been water baptized. This is the real significance of water baptism. It is a public testimony that a person has received Jesus Christ as their savior and Lord by repentance and faith in the gospel (Acts 2:41). It is an external, public demonstration of what has happened in the heart when a person receives the word (Acts 2:41). In some cultures, public water baptism leads to rejection by the family, persecution, and sometimes death by martyrdom.

Infant Baptism

There is no biblical justification in the New Testament for baptizing infants. The only implications that infants are baptized are the statements "she and her household had been baptized" (Acts 16:15), which was spoken about Lydia, and "he was baptized, he and all his household" (Acts 16:33), which was spoken about the Philippian jailer, both in Acts chapter 16. It is suggested that there may have been infants in one of the households mentioned, but there is no evidence for that fact. Rather, in every other recorded instance of water baptism there is the act of believing, recieving and then water baptism (Acts 8:34–39). The clear implication is that a person has the maturity to understand the gospel and make a conscious choice to either receive or reject salvation in Jesus Christ. Then, after receiving Jesus as savior and Lord, water baptism follows. An infant does not have the maturity to do this.

Infant baptism seems to arise from the concern that infants are not under grace and will go to hell if not baptized by sprinkling with water. There are several biblical references that contradict this teaching. Job 3:16–19 clearly teaches that even the unborn child goes to be with God in heaven. This is also confirmed in Ecclesiastes 4:3 and Ecclesiastes 6:3–6, which teach that an infant dying in the womb is better off than a life lived without a relationship with God. David points out in II Samuel 12:23 that his young child that died has gone to be with God by saying, "I will go to him, but he will not return to me." An age of accountability seems to be the factor in determining when God holds a child accountable for personal sin. In the Old Testament it is 19 years of age, as pointed out in Numbers 14:28–31 and Deuteronomy 1:39. In the New Testament it is 12 years old as shown in Mark 5:36–43 and Luke 8:40–56. In this case Jesus said the little girl was sleeping when she had actually died. Sleeping in death is only mentioned in the context of someone who belongs to God by faith or was still under the grace of God as a child (John 11:11; Mark 5:39; I Corinthians 11:30; I Thessalonians 4:13). The age of accountability before God for personal sin is not suggested to be either 12 or 19 years of age. Rather, it is more likely that it depends on the person and the love and wisdom of God. For a mentally retarded person it may be a lifetime. Only God has the capability to determine such matters. It is comforting to realize whatever He does is good. As a final thought on this subject, consider Paul's comment about himself:

The Wind That Never Changes

> I was once alive once apart from the Law; but when the commandment came, sin became alive and I died. (Romans 7:9)

In this verse, Paul is referring to innocence in childhood when he was unaware of God's commandments and incapable of understanding what they meant to him personally. At some point his willful, self-centered sin nature dominated his life, and he died to his innocence. It is not known when this transformation happened for Paul or for any of us. At some point in all our lives we become enemies of God (Romans 5:10). It is probably at different times for different people. However, at some point God holds us accountable for sin. Before that point, known only to God, a person is under His grace. This is the clear teaching of scripture.

Infant baptism is a carryover from the covenant of circumcision which God gave to Abraham (Genesis 17:10). It is practiced not only to insure the infant is under the grace of God and is going to heaven, but also as a ceremony for the parents to covenant before God to bring the child up in the ways of God. A dedication ceremony is not an unscriptural thing to have. Including a water baptism by sprinkling for an infant to commemorate the occasion does no harm. Many parents see it exactly this way, as a ceremony to dedicate the child to God and to trust God that they will raise the child to know God and for His service. The parents need to realize the child is already under the grace of God, as has been discussed. They also need to realize that the child will need to become a Christian by personally responding to the gospel when they get older, and then being water baptized by immersion as Jesus commanded.

Immersion or Sprinkling

With regard to the method of believer's baptism, it is clear that the judgment of God was not sprinkled on Jesus on the cross. As has been pointed out, Jesus was under the "waves and billows" of God's judgment for us (Psalm 42:7). Since water baptism is a representation of what happened on the cross, immersion is the correct method. However, while immersion is the correct biblical method, being sprinkled as a believer with the right heart attitude is more pleasing to God than being immersed with the wrong attitude. As stated in the beginning of this essay, with God it is always about the heart (Psalm 51:16–17).

Summary

As an insightful summary of the doctrine of baptism, consider what Paul the apostle reveals in the following passage:

> For I do not want you to be unaware, brethren, that our fathers were all under the cloud and all passed through the sea; and all were baptized into Moses in the cloud and in the sea; and all ate the same spiritual food; and all drank the same spiritual drink, for they were drinking from a spiritual rock which followed them; and the rock was Christ. (I Corinthians 10:1-4)

This passage of scripture reveals that the nation of Israel was baptized into Moses in the cloud and in the sea. It is a clear teaching in the Old Testament that Moses was a type or prefigure of Christ (Deuteronomy 18:15), and the nation of Israel was a type or prefigure of a New Testament believer (I Corinthians 10:1-10). Following the story of Israel's redemption by blood in Exodus through their entering into Canaan in the book of Joshua is a picture of the Christian life from salvation by faith (rooted) to maturity and victory (grounded).(Ephesians 3:17).

In years of careful study and meditation on the Holy Scriptures (Isaian 28:9-10), the Holy Spirit will eventually reveal to the true child of God the amazing truths and mysteries that are contained in the Old Testament. Someone has said, "The Old Testament is the New Testament contained and the New Testament is the Old Testament explained." Mysteries of how God trains and disciplines every child He receives are to be found in the Old Testament. As brief examples, we see death, burial and resurrection in the lives of Abraham, Joseph, Moses, and

David, just to mention a few. We see weakness, betrayal, failure, and character flaws that God turned into victory for His glory and purpose. We see God's use of time and how He is working in lives when it appears He is doing nothing. It is not accidental that approximately 70 percent of the Bible is the Old Testament. It could be said that a measure of biblical maturity occurs when the believer develops a love and appreciation for the Old Testament that is equal to their love and appreciation of the New Testament. We learn how our Heavenly Father deals with His children in the Old Testament. We learn His ways (Hebrews 3:10).

If we consider the nation of Israel from Egypt to Canaan as told from the books of Exodus to Joshua, we gain some insights into New Testament salvation. First of all, Israel's salvation was in God's timing and way. He sent Moses to Israel with the message of redemption accompanied by signs and wonders, as in the book of Acts (Acts 5:12). Like us, Israel did not believe at first (Exodus 5:21), but God kept pursuing and carrying our His plan until they did believe enough to get delivered. However, they had a long way to go in the believing area before they were ready for spiritual warfare. That preparation took over forty years. As was discussed in the life of Abraham earlier, Israel was *rooted* in the love of God the night they believed Him by staying under the blood (Exodus 12:21–28). Israel was *grounded* in the love of God over forty years later when they believed God would deliver them from strong enemies (Joshua 1:16–17).

Following the story starting in Exodus 12:1, Moses tells the nation of Israel, "This month shall be the beginning of months to you." This is the beginning of your national life. New life starts this month. A new life and a new calendar. Sounds like "born again" (John 3:7). He then tells them what to do for Passover night. Kill a certain animal and put some of its blood on the outside door side posts and lintel. When the death angel passes through the land to kill the first born in every household it will pass over any house that has the blood (Exodus 12:13). Israel was saved by blood. It was a type of how Christians are saved by the blood of Christ.(Romans 5:9).

The next major event in Israel's salvation experience is that God manifests His Presence in the form of a cloud by day and pillar of fire by night, visible to the whole nation of Israel (Exodus 13:21–22). It happens the day after they were saved by blood. This represents the baptism by the Holy Spirit for the New Testament believer.(I Corinthians 12:13). The first thing that happens after someone repents and believes in Jesus is baptism by the Holy Spirit to seal the believer (Ephesians 1:13). This does not mean the believer is mature or completely controlled by the Holy Spirit. It is the new life of Christ imparted to the believer by the Holy Spirit, as discussed earlier. It is what makes a believer born again with a new life. Learning to walk and live in power by drinking the Holy Spirit (I Corinthians 12:13) day by day is something that must be learned and exercised (Hebrews 5:14). This is why it took Abraham twenty-five years and Israel forty years to go from rooted to grounded in the love of God (Ephesians 3:17). Christian maturity is not instant (Hebrews 6:1-3; I Timothy 3:6).

Thus far in Israel's salvation experience there has been salvation by blood and baptism by the Holy Spirit. The next item in God's plan is water baptism for the whole nation. He leads them into what looks like an impossible situation, with mountains surrounding them, a sea in front of them, and an Egyptian army coming in the only escape route to kill most of them and bring them back into captivity (Exodus 14:1–4). God tells them to go forward (Exodus 14:15). God puts the pillar of fire between Israel and the Egyptians all night while He opens a path through the Red sea. In the morning the entire nation walks through the midst of the Red sea on dry land with walls of water on their left and right. They went down below the surface of the water and came back up the other side: baptism in the sea, just like Paul said (I Corinthians 10:2). After Israel gets to the other shore, God removes the pillar of fire and the Egyptian army pursues Israel into the path through the sea. When the army is in the midst of the sea, God causes the water to return and all the army drowns.

There are two significant points that must be made about Israel's national baptism:

1. In the waters of baptism their former taskmasters were killed. For the Christian, the worst, most ruthless taskmaster is the sin nature. Humans have no power against the sin nature. No amount of self-sacrifice can deal with the sin nature (Colossians 2:23). Only God can deal with the sin nature by putting it to death. He accomplishes this in Jesus on the cross as has been discussed. Water baptism represents this reality that happens on the cross.

2. The Red sea was a physical separation between Israel and their old life in Egypt. It represents the fact that, in Christ, the believer is dead to the world and the world is dead to the believer (Galatians 6:14). This is the second expression of water baptism that happens through the cross: separation from the world.

Israel was out of Egypt but Egypt was not out of Israel. They bring it up every time things get a little hard for the next 40 years (Exodus 16:3). It took God forty years of discipline and training to get Egypt out of Israel (Joshua 5:9). This is what it means to grow up as a Christian: obeying and trusting God to transform us from worldliness to Christlikeness. It takes a long time but it is so worth it to know Him and give Him glory by growing in Him (Philippians 3:7–16).

So here is the order for New Testament conversion as pictured by Israel:

1. salvation through blood by faith
2. receiving the Holy Spirit
3. being water baptized by immersion
4. learning to live in the Power of the Holy Spirit by drinking the Holy Spirit every moment of every day (I Corinthians

12:13).

There is much more that can be learned about the Christian life by studying how God dealt with Israel from Egypt to Canaan, but that is for Essay III.

ESSAY III

Spirit of Truth

Introduction

Who is the Holy Spirit? How does the Holy Spirit interact with human beings? What are the goals of the Holy Spirit?

These questions will be answered in this essay.

God is spirit, and those who worship Him must worship in spirit and truth (John 4:24). This verse has two realities that challenge human understanding: spirit and truth. *Spirit* is not bounded by our four dimensional understanding of space and time. It is transcendent. Similarly, absolute, immutable, eternal *truth* is also transcendent. Traditionally, truth is acceptance of a fact or standard. A problem arises: Society establishes the acceptance of fact or standard. Historically, what was a fact yesterday, such as "we understand all the energy in the universe," is not a fact today. What was a standard in the past, such as certain rules of societal behavior, are not accepted today. Commonly, truth is actually knowledge—knowledge that is evolving and incomplete. This is not a bad thing. Science, medicine, and all forms of human understanding should be evolving and continually improving, as they have throughout history. However, this process of constant learning and updating demonstrates that human knowledge is not absolute, immutable, eternal truth.

Always learning and never able to come to the knowledge of the truth (II Timothy 3:7). Notice the two words *never able*. This sums up the problem when it comes to humans and eternal truth. Fallen human nature cannot understand or experience Truth. Salvation in Jesus Christ, as discussed in Essays I and II, includes new life in the Holy Spirit that illumines the sin-darkened human heart and imparts eternal life to the human spirit. Only when the human heart is transformed from darkness to light by the power of God and the human spirit is made alive in Jesus Christ, can a person begin to understand and know the Truth. Truth is a Person, the Lord Jesus Christ. He is the embodiment and revelation of Truth to the human heart by the Holy Spirit. Jesus Christ is the Word of God that reveals the will of God that shows the wisdom of God in the work of God. The cross expresses the work of God. "For the word of the cross is foolishness to those who are perishing, but to us who are being saved it is the power of God" (I Corinthians 1:18).

The Wind That Never Changes

God imparts truth to the human heart by the process of revelation. It does not come by study and learning. *Revelation* is the divine or supernatural disclosure to humans of something relating to human existence in the spiritual realm that was previously unknown. It is much more than information or facts. The apostle Paul gives the Source of all his knowledge of truth that he preached in his lifetime and wrote down for future generations: "For I neither received it from man, nor was I taught it, but I received it through a revelation of Jesus Christ" (Galatians 1:12). When Peter made his great confession that Jesus was the Christ, the son of the living God, Jesus answered, "Blessed are you, Simon Barjona, because flesh and blood did not reveal this to you, but my Father who is in heaven" (Matthew 16:17). No one knows the truth of God in Jesus Christ apart from revelation by the Spirit of Truth. Revealed knowledge from God about Jesus Christ is transformative. It changes everything.

This essay discusses the ministry of the Spirit of Truth. In addition to *common grace*, "life and breath and all things" (Acts 17:25), which is given by the Holy Spirit to all living humans at all times, there is *redemptive grace*: "For by grace you have been saved; and that not of yourselves, it is the gift of God" (Ephesians 2:8). These activities of the Holy Spirit lead a person to salvation and new life in Jesus Christ. The beginning of this ministry is the Holy Spirit wooing or drawing a person's heart to repentance and faith in Jesus: "No one can come to me unless the Father who sent Me draws him; and I will raise him up on the last day" (John 6:44). God initiates salvation. No one on his own initiative seeks God: "There is none who understands, there is none who seeks for God" (Romans 3:11). Salvation in Jesus Christ requires death to self and absolute, total surrender of one's life to the Lordship of Jesus Christ. It is not characteristic of human nature to seek death to self and totally give up control of one's life. The Holy Spirit reveals to a person's mind and heart the hopeless, helpless, utterly lost condition of one's soul that leads to a desperate crying out to God for mercy and grace in Jesus Christ. To come to this place of brokenness and humility takes the grace of God. It is a gift. No one can come to this place on their own. Repentance and faith are gifts from God by the Holy Spirit. No person who is truly born again by the Holy Spirit takes any credit or has any pride in anything they did to merit God's salvation. They humbly acknowledge that God did it all and they know Him only because of His mercy and grace. It is not about seeking what a person can do for God, but rather about believing and receiving what He has done for us in Jesus Christ. Essays I and II discuss God's salvation in considerable detail. This present Essay on the Spirit of Truth deals with the ministry of the Holy Spirit to the believing Christian.

The Holy Spirit Is a Person

In the Scriptures, there are many actions and characteristics of the Holy Spirit. The Holy Spirit creates, reveals, inspires, seals, teaches, helps, comforts, anoints, testifies, transports, empowers, sees, speaks, leads, heals, does supernatural acts, gives visions and dreams, and is manifested as, or likened to wind, fire, water and a dove. These actions and characteristics are in both the Old and New Testaments. In the Old Testament, believers had the Holy Spirit with or upon them. In the New Testament, after the cross and the resurrection of Jesus, the Holy Spirit takes up residence or dwells in a believer. As Jesus explained to His disciples, "The Spirit of Truth whom the world cannot receive, because it does not see Him or know Him, but you know Him because He abides with you and will be in you" (John 14:17). After Jesus ascended into Heaven, He sent the promised Holy Spirit to dwell in believers as discussed in Acts chapter 2. From this point on in the history of Christianity, all true believers have the gift of the Holy Spirit after they repent and receive Jesus as discussed in Essays I and II.

The Holy Spirit's relations with humans in the New Testament are less common in the Old Testament. In the New Testament, the Holy Spirit is specifically described as being grieved, resisted, quenched, jealous, loving, insulted, lied to, and blasphemed. These characteristics and the ones previously discussed are consistent with a personal, interactive, involved, relational God who desires fellowship with human beings. Jesus defines eternal life as a relationship: "This is eternal life, that they many know You, the only true God, and Jesus Christ whom You have sent" (John 17:3). The word *know* in this verse means an intimate relationship as in between two close friends or as in the marriage relationship between a man and woman. It is not a casual relationship. Eternal life in Jesus Christ is now in this life. We do not have to wait until we die and go into God's presence. The Holy Spirit is an eternal Gift to the believer in Jesus Christ so we can experience God in this life and have a real relationship with Him as with any person.

> However, you are not in the flesh but the Spirit, if indeed the Spirit of God dwells in you. But if anyone does not have the Spirit of Christ, he does not belong to Him. If Christ is in you, though the body is dead because of sin, yet the spirit is alive because of righteousness. But if the Spirit of Him who raised Jesus from the dead dwells in you, He who raised Christ Jesus from the dead will also give life to your mortal body through His Spirit who dwells in you. (Romans 8:9–11)

Notice in these verses that God the Father, God the Son, and God the Holy Spirit are all three in the context of being in the Spirit. If you have the Holy Spirit, you have the Spirit of the Father and the Spirit of the Son as well. This is a mystery. We accept it by faith.

The default mode of the unregenerate human heart with regard to religion is being good and not being bad. The human thought is that God insists that a person be good if they want to please Him. Holy Scripture does not support this line of reasoning. In fact, God has said, "There is none who does good, there is not even one" (Romans 3:12). God has made a way for human beings to enter into a living, eternal relationship with Him through the life, death, burial, and resurrection of Jesus Christ —not on the goodness or lack of badness of the human, but on the mercy and grace of God. Jesus said, "I am the good shepherd, and I know My own, and My own know Me, even as the Father knows Me, and I know the Father; and I lay down My life for the sheep" (John 10:14-15). The amazing revelation in these verses is that God the Father desires that we as humans know Jesus and Jesus knows us as Jesus and the Father know each other. This supernatural relationship completely depends on God and not on us. He is the Initiator and we are the responder. He takes the active role and we take the passive role. We cannot understand this relationship intellectually but with the heart. God has to reveal to us by the Holy Spirit how to enter into such a supernatural relationship and how to grow in that relationship.

This is the essence of true Christianity: a relationship with God that is moment-by-moment, living, active, developing, enjoyed, embraced, cultivated, and filled with mutual communications and interactions between two friends. It is everything an intimate relationship between two intelligent beings should be. It is fulfilling, thrilling, satisfying, comforting, exciting, and definitely not boring. It is a relationship based on the supernatural love of God as described in I Corinthians chapter 13. Based on love, it is also full of emotion and sometimes passion. All through the scriptures from Genesis to Revelation God expresses and demonstrates emotion and passion in His relationship with His children. His children regularly express and demonstrate emotion and passion towards God as in the Psalms, The Song of Solomon, and many other scriptures. These interactions between God and His children express the full range of emotion and passion in a relationship: devotion, commitment, serving, giving, submission, sacrifice, expressions of love and tenderness, jealousy, hurt, and even anger. This is a real relationship, not an empty, lifeless routine of ritual and rules.

God's greatest desire in both the Old and New Testaments is for humans to love Him. Jesus said, the greatest commandment in the Old Testament is "You shall love the Lord your God with all your heart and with all your soul and with all your might" (Deuteronomy 6:5). A little meditation on this verse should conclude that to love God like this is impossible. This is the point of the Law of Moses. We are to realize we cannot do it (Galatians 3:24). In the New Testament, love is on a higher level—a level that does not depend on human effort. In the New Testament God does not command us to love Him. He gives us perfect love for Him by the Holy Spirit: "The love of God has been poured out within our hearts through the Holy Spirit who was given to us" (Romans 5:5). This means that God's perfect love between the three Persons of the Godhead and His perfect love for humans has been poured out in our hearts when we received the Holy Spirit. This is a stunning reality: *We can love like God because we have the Holy Spirit.* In the New Testament we are not commanded to love others like we love ourselves as in the Old Testament (Leviticus 19:18). Jesus gave us a new commandment: "A new commandment I give to you, that you love one another, even as I have loved you, that you also love one another" (John 13:34). The Christian life is a lifetime process of learning to love God and others with God's perfect love. This is in more detail in the section on "The Foundation of Love."

In conclusion, the Holy Spirit brings to our heart and life the fullness of God in His love and holy character (Ephesians 3:19). The Holy Spirit enables us and leads us into a living relationship with a personal, loving God. The Holy Spirit is the very essence of God's Person because He is God Himself. Only humans created in God's image have the innate spiritual capacity to enter into such a relationship. This is a mystery. In this life we are not permitted to understand how all this happens. Our response to the mercy and grace of God is to believe and receive His salvation in Jesus Christ. It is an adventure like no other.

The Holy Spirit in Salvation

Since the Holy Spirit is a Person He communicates with human beings according to His own will. The methods He uses to communicate are many and varied. He uses sickness (Job 33:16–30), adversity (Psalm 142:6), supernatural signs (Acts 13:8–12), dreams (Genesis 37:5–7), visions (Acts 16:9), speaking with an audible voice or directly to the mind (Acts 9:3–8;

Acts 8:29), impressions (Acts 27:10), circumstances (Acts 16:7) and other people (Acts 21:11). This list is not exhaustive with regard to how the Holy Spirit communicates. When it comes to salvation, the Holy Spirit is seeking to get a person's attention, and He often will use the methods just listed. He needs to get our attention because fallen human nature is not looking for God and His salvation. We think we are, but we are not because we have no idea what we are looking for.

> God has looked down from heaven upon the sons of men to see if there is anyone who understands, who seeks after God. Every one of them has turned aside; together they have become corrupt; there is no one who does good, not even one. (Psalm 53:2–3).

Only God is good (Luke 18:19). Humans have no idea what good really means. Therefore, all humans everywhere come up with their own ideas of what it means to be good (Romans 10:3). They blindly go on through life completely unaware that they are totally missing what it means to seek after or to know God. This is why the Holy Spirit must first get our attention. He has to bring us up short and stop us on our current mad dash through life so we can begin to hear what He wants to say to us (Romans 3:19).

Once the Holy Spirit has our attention, the primary way He speaks to us is the Word of God or the Bible. The Holy Spirit wrote the Bible. He used men to pen the words but the scriptures clearly teach that the Holy Spirit is the Author (II Peter 1:21). Because the Bible is a supernatural book, it is "living and active" (Hebrews 4:12). The Holy Spirit begins to reveal to us by the Word of God who Jesus is and what He has done for us. He also reveals our true state of being as hopeless sinners who desperately need a savior. He imparts faith to the human heart (Romans 12:3; I Corinthians 12:9; Ephesians 2:8). The revelation of the Word and the impartation of faith are gifts from God. It is impossible to come to the correct understanding of Jesus and His salvation without the help of the Holy Spirit. Jesus said "No one can come to me unless the Father Who sent me draws

The Wind That Never Changes

him; and I will raise him up on the last day" (John 6:44).

This process of revelation and impartation of faith leading to repentance, believing, and receiving Jesus as Savior and Lord is the work of the Holy Spirit in drawing a person to the Person of Jesus Christ. He uses supernatural Words from God to accomplish this:

> And he will speak words to you by which you will be saved, you and your household. (Acts 11:14)

> Men of Israel, listen to these words: Jesus the Nazarene, a man attested to you by God with miracles and wonders and signs which God performed through Him in your midst, just as you yourselves know.... (Acts 2:22)

The ministry of the Holy Spirit when Jesus walked the earth is the same as it is today: to bear witness that Jesus is the Christ the Son of the living God. The Holy Spirit does not draw attention to Himself. He draws attention to Jesus: "No one can say, 'Jesus is Lord,' except by the Holy Spirit" (I Corinthians 12:3); "When the Helper comes, whom I will send to you from the Father, He will testify about Me" (John 15:26).

It is important to realize that the Holy Spirit, while never changing His work of revealing and glorifying Jesus, does not deal with each believer in the same way. Historically, it has been sadly common for a person to conclude that their particular revelation of God's salvation is the one and only method to salvation. For example, some people experience great emotion in the salvation experience. Others feel no particular emotion at all. Therefore, the people that experience emotion believe and teach that emotion is a necessary manifestation of salvation. This is not biblical. Nowhere in the scripture does it teach that emotions are necessary as proof of salvation. Jesus said, "you will know them by their fruits" (Matthew 7:16). Does the life of a professing believer in Jesus Christ glorify Jesus by manifesting His love, character, and obedience? This is the true and only evidence of salvation. Emotions inspired by the Holy Spirit are wonderful, transcendent, and life changing. However, the Holy Spirit gives emotional experiences and revelations as it pleases Him. We walk by faith, not by sight (II Corinthians 5:7). *Sight* can mean anything that we perceive as proofs of God's approval or presence in our life. This is not biblical. His promises are our confidence and joy.

> Grace and peace be multiplied to you in the knowledge of God and of Jesus our Lord; seeing that His divine power has granted to us everything pertaining to life and godliness, through the true knowledge of Him who called us by His own glory and excellence. For by these He has granted to us His precious and magnificent promises, so that by them you may become partakers of the divine nature, having escaped the corruption that is in the world by lust. (II Peter 1:2–4)

A careful study and meditation on the book of Acts also illustrates the different ways the Holy Spirit brings believers to repentance and faith in Jesus. On the day of Pentecost in Acts 2 there were great and powerful manifestations of the Holy Spirit of wind, fire, and speaking in tongues. In Acts 3 the Holy Spirit used a miracle of healing to get the attention of the people so they could hear and receive the Word about Jesus. Same Holy Spirit, same message, same result, different methods. In Acts 10 God sent an angel to appear to Cornelius to send for Peter and hear words from him. Peter came and preached the Word and all in the house received Jesus as Savior and spoke in tongues. In Acts 13 Paul preached a message and many believed in the grace of God and followed Paul and Barnabas. In Acts 16 Paul preached to a group of women by a river. The Holy Spirit opened the heart of a woman named Lydia and she believed. In these last two examples, no mention is made of supernatural manifestations, emotions, or speaking in tongues.

The Holy Spirit uses the Word of God to change hearts. This is true all through the book of Acts in different accounts of salvation in Jesus. Sometimes there are supernatural manifestations, sometimes there are none. Sometimes there are emotions as specifically mentioned in Acts 8:39 for the Ethiopian, and sometimes the conversion experience is quiet as in Acts 16:14–15 for Lydia. It is very important to place the emphasis on the fact of the mercy and grace of God as revealed by the Holy Spirit, rather than dwell on how the Holy Spirit chose to reveal that mercy and grace. If Lydia, Cornelius, and the Ethiopian were to meet and share their testimonies, the emphasis would be on the joy of knowing Jesus instead of how it happened. This may appear to be obvious. However, one of the reasons for so much division in the modern church is the reaction to and interpretation of how the Holy Spirit works in bringing different people to Jesus. In the book of Acts, the only event that most consistently happened in each salvation experience is water baptism. Essay II covers the subject of water baptism. In summary, the Holy Spirit 1. reveals (Matthew 16:17), 2. draws (John 6:44), 3. convicts (John 16:8), 4. grants repentance (II Timothy 2:25), 5. gives the gift of faith (Romans 12:3), 6. seals (Ephesians 1:13) and 7. empowers (Acts 1:8) a believer in Jesus Christ. This is the beginning of an eternal journey with God.

The Foundation of Love

> The one who does not love does not know God, for God is love. (I John 4:8)

> Beloved, let us love one another, for love is from God; and everyone who loves is born of God and knows God. (I John 4:7)

> We have come to know and have believed the love which God has for us. God is love, and the one who abides in love abides in God and God abides in Him. (I John 4:16)

There is no clearer revelation in the scriptures than the importance and centrality of love. Paul says to Timothy, "The goal of our instruction is love from a pure heart" (I Timothy 1:5). Peter gives a list of desirable qualities for the Christian with the pinnacle being love (II Peter 1:5–7). Paul tells us that no matter how we are spiritually gifted, how much faith we have, how much knowledge we have, or if we die a martyr's death, it must be motivated and actuated by love. Otherwise, it is useless (I Corinthians 13:1–3). The phrases *fullness of God* and *fullness of Christ*, as applied to believers, occur only two times in all the scriptures. Both are in the context of knowing the supernatural love of Christ, (Ephesians 3:14–21; 4:11–16).

Given these scriptures and many others like them in the New Testament, one would think that emphasizing the love of God would be the central theme of Christianity. Sadly, this is not the case. All too often doctrinal issues divide Christians. A good illustration of how this has happened is in a book titled *The Heavenly Man* by Brother Yun (1). Brother Yun's book covers the development of Chinese house churches from the early 1970's up until about 2000. When China's borders started opening up in the 1980's, foreign Christians started smuggling Bibles into China. In the beginning, this was so helpful and appreciated by the Chinese house churches. There was much love and unity among all the house church groups. Later, there were other books included along with the Bibles. These books were about various denominations' theology, teachings on tongues, roles of women in the church, and other secondary teachings. The Chinese Christians read all these books and became confused. Eventually, various groups began to identify with specific teachings and each group considered the way they believed was the only right way. This trend continued for several years until the Chinese house churches divided into ten or more segments. Leaders in each segment would not fellowship or have anything to do with leaders in other segments. Each group considered themselves right on certain doctrines and thought of the other groups as cults. Over time, the preaching of Jesus included criticism of other groups. Love and unity no longer existed among all the Chinese house church groups.

From the beginning of the China house-church movement in 1970, there had been severe persecution. This had not prevented the amazing growth of the church in China or dim the passionate love Chinese believers had for Jesus and each other. Persecution did not diminish the manifestation of God's love or divide the church. The church experienced division because they did not seek first the Main Thing. It is clear in the New Testament that the Main Thing is Jesus and His love. Doctrine is

The Wind That Never Changes

important, faith is important, knowledge is important, power and supernatural manifestations are important, but none of these is the Main Thing.

Jesus said,

> By this all men will know that you are my disciples, if you have love for one another. (John 13:35)

and

> I in them and You in Me, that they may be perfected in unity, so that the world may know that You sent Me, and loved them, even as You have loved Me. (John 17:23)

In these two verses, Jesus gives us the only two evidences in all of scripture that demonstrate to the world that believers are his disciples and that He was sent by the Father: love and unity. This is the heart of Christianity and the ministry of the Holy Spirit. Paul makes it very clear in all his writings that love, resulting in unity among believers, is the Main Thing.

It needs to be recognized and regularly acknowledged that human beings fall into comfort zones and familiar patterns. When it comes to spiritual revelation, the natural tendency is to conclude that the ways the Holy Spirit reveals things to me are the right and best ways. Pride is inevitably at the core of this problem. It has been said, "Pride is the most stubborn root that grows in the heart of man." Somehow, humans get it into their thinking and, most importantly, in their emotions that the way they see it is the right way. The default mode of the human heart is pride. Only the power of the Holy Spirit can bring a human heart to a place of humility and brokenness before God and in relationship with others. Love and unity are not common in human relationships. It takes the power of God.

This is evident in the scriptures beginning with Cain and Able in Genesis 4:8 right on up to the last great battle recorded in Revelation 19:19. Pride is the first sin recorded in eternity (Isaiah 14:13-14). The created chose to exercise his will in opposition to the Creator. This was the fall of Lucifer, Son of the Morning. His downfall was pride. Today we call him Satan. He uses pride to deceive human hearts that they know best, even in opposition to the infinite Creator. If he fails in keeping humans away from humility and brokenness in repentance before God, he tries to divide the children of God using religion, doctrine, tradition, music, gifts of the Spirit, and many other devices. The only antidote to this slippery slope is regularly seeking the face of God. When we humble ourselves and cultivate our relationship with our Heavenly Father through Jesus Christ in the power of the Holy Spirit, the Holy Spirit will reveal our heart to us by the Word and the Spirit (Hebrews 4:12; II Corinthians 3:18). It requires constant diligence to allow the Spirit of God to keep us on track (Hebrews 4:11). The track that we must stay on is the love of God. The Apostle Paul emphasizes this track in the book of Ephesians. After discussing salvation by faith in Jesus Christ and sealing by the Holy Spirit, Paul mentions the first of two prayers he has for the Ephesians:

> That the God of our Lord Jesus Christ, the Father of glory, may give to you a spirit of wisdom and of revelation in the knowledge of Him. I pray that the eyes of your heart may be enlightened, so that you will know what is the hope of His calling, what are the riches of the glory of His inheritance in the saints, and what is the surpassing greatness of His power toward us who believe. (Ephesians 1:17-19)

Paul is writing to Christians who are born again and have a relationship with Jesus. Yet, his prayer starts with the request that they may receive from God a spirit of wisdom and revelation in the knowledge of Jesus—a knowledge that they do not presently possess. This is an ongoing process in the life of a believer in Jesus—ever increasing knowledge by revelation of the hope, glory, and power of what it means to be a child of God through faith in Jesus.

The second of Paul's prayers for the Ephesians again appears to make an unexpected request:

> For this reason I bow my knees before the Father, from whom every family in heaven and on earth derives its name, that He would grant you, according to the riches of His glory, to be strengthened with power through

> His Spirit in the inner man, so that Christ may dwell in your hearts through faith; and that you, being rooted and grounded in love, may be able to comprehend with all the saints what is the breadth and length and height and depth, and to know the love of Christ which surpasses knowledge, that you may be filled up to all the fullness of God. (Ephesians 3:14-19)

Paul prays that Christ may dwell in their hearts through faith. As Christians, Christ already dwells in their hearts according to Romans 8:9. Similar to the prayer in Ephesians chapter 1, Paul is praying for a deeper, more comprehensive experience of the significance of Christ dwelling in the heart of a believer. It is a reference to the ongoing filling of the Holy Spirit, "be strengthened with power through His Spirit in the inner man." Paul is teaching that it is not only biblical but also desirable that believers ask for more of the Holy Spirit to strengthen them. For what reason? That Christ will dwell in them to a greater and greater extent to the end that they be rooted and grounded in His supernatural love along with all other believers: love and unity in His body.

The word *dwell* in the original Greek means "the Presence of Divine power and influence to pervade, prompt, and govern attitudes and actions in the life of a believer." A. W. Tozer called this process *The Divine Conquest*. It begins when a person receives Jesus as :their Savior and Lord and continues throughout life as an ongoing process that never ends. It is a growing relationship between a finite being and an infinite Being.

It cannot be accomplished in one lifetime. It will take an eternity. However, it is God's constant and consistent intention that His children continue to grow in the grace and knowledge of Him (Ephesians 4:15). As Paul concludes, the goal is to "be filled up to all the fullness of God." This specific phrase *the fullness of God* occurs one more time in Ephesians 4:13 as "the fullness of Christ." In both places, the context and the Greek meaning of the word translated *fullness* refers to the collective Church or Body of Christ. In other words, no one person can contain all the fullness of God. However, the collective Body of

Christ can contain and express the fullness of God as a group.

One example of the meaning of the Greek word Paul used for *fullness* is how a ship is full of sailors. It takes all the sailors to fill the ship. Similarly, it takes the entire Body of Christ—past, present, and future—to contain and express the fullness of God in Christ. This is the mystery of Christ being the Head and the Church being the Body (Colossians 1:18). Considering Paul's discussion when comparing the Church to a human body in I Corinthians 12:12-27, it should be obvious that love and unity are two foundational principles of Christianity. Supernatural love imparted to the human heart by the indwelling Holy Spirit is the means by which an individual believer in Jesus loves God and his fellow believers. Since "love covers a multitude of sins" (I Peter 4:8), it is also the means by which the Body of Christ achieves unity. Apart from Jesus, all human beings are broken, flawed, and imperfect. Even after being in Christ for decades, we still occasionally manifest the fruit of the flesh in pride and other ways. As James 3:2 says, "In many ways we all stumble." We all constantly need mercy and grace from God our Father and our fellow believers. This is why the Church of Jesus Christ is unique in human experience.

Filled with the Holy Spirit

Few subjects in New Testament Christianity are as confusing and controversial as the filling of the Holy Spirit. It is very difficult, even with a thorough knowledge and understanding of Scripture, to formalize a concise theology of how God chooses to manifest His Presence and power in one of His children. Few subjects elicit an emotional reaction in a believer like the filling of the Holy Spirit. Why is this the case? Because each one of us has his own experience to draw on with regard to how the Holy Spirit came to him. Therefore, we strongly tend to interpret the teaching of scripture on the Holy Spirit to fit our particular experience. That experience ranges from no particular experience to a supernatural experience, and everything in

The Wind That Never Changes

between. Consequently, the no-particular-experience believers look on the supernatural-experience believers as emotional and unstable. The supernatural-experience believers look on the no-particular-experience believers as shallow and unspiritual. Both groups feel fully justified in their positions by their understanding of scripture. This is an unfortunate dilemma. Sadly, love does not play a major role in this controversy.

Two thoughts on biblical interpretation are necessary before this discussion begins: First, "All Scripture is inspired by God and profitable for teaching, for reproof, for correction, for training in righteousness" (II Timothy 3:16). It is axiomatic that all Scriptures from Genesis to Revelation are on an equal status with regard to importance. Some believers hold that the four Gospels have greater validity and authority than the rest of Scripture because they record Words spoken by Jesus when He was on earth. *Scripture itself does not support this position.* There are many examples throughout the entire Old Testament of God speaking Words directly, such as to the entire nation of Israel at Mount Sinai when He spoke the Ten Commandments (Exodus 20). The book of Job records God speaking His Words. Psalms and many of the prophetic books reveal the Words of God directly spoken to a human being.

> But know this first of all, that no prophecy of Scripture is a matter of one's own interpretation, for no prophecy was ever made by an act of human will, but men moved by the Holy Spirit spoke from God. (II Peter 1: 20–21)

The second thought is the role of Paul the Apostle as being the most prolific writer in the New Testament. Similar to Moses writing the Law in the Old Testament, the Holy Spirit revealed the theology of New Testament salvation to Paul, as he confesses in II Corinthians 12:7. The Lord choose Paul not only to suffer for His Name as an Apostle, evangelist, and teacher, but also to record for all generations practical doctrine and theology on New Testament salvation that are not clearly revealed in the four Gospels or the book of Acts. The Holy Spirit inspired every Word that Paul wrote as He also inspired all the words written by all writers of Old and New Testament Scriptures. Since the Holy Spirit is the Author of the entire Bible, everything Paul wrote is in perfect agreement with all other Scripture. Even in Paul's lifetime, the other Apostles recognized his writings as Scripture (II Peter 3:15-16). This is important because Paul's writings give details about the Holy Spirit that are not included in the Gospels or Acts. It is common for many believers to develop their entire theology and doctrine about the Holy Spirit from only the Gospels or the book of Acts. This is problematic, because a complete picture of how the Holy Spirit ministers His Presence and Power is only possible by taking into account all the scriptures on the subject.

Several foundational points are derived from I Corinthians 12:13 regarding how the Holy Spirit ministers to believers in Jesus Christ:

> For by one Spirit we were all baptized into one body, whether Jews or Greeks, whether slaves or free, and we were all made to drink of one Spirit. (I Corinthians 12:13)

First, to whom does this verse apply? Paul uses the phrase *we were all* two times. In many other scriptures, Paul uses the term *we all* when he wants to emphasize the fact that what he is talking about applies universally to all believers. It does not matter about ethnicity or social status. The principles in this verse apply to all believers equally, including Paul himself. In this verse, Paul reveals two ministries of the Holy Spirit to the believer.

First, we were all baptized into one body by the Holy Spirit. This is the baptism that John the Baptist spoke of when referring to Jesus: "He who is coming after me is mightier than I, and I am not fit to remove His sandals; He will baptize you with the Holy Spirit and fire" (Matthew 3:11). Jesus spoke of this same baptism: "For John baptized with water, but you will be baptized with the Holy Spirit not many days from now" (Acts 1:5). Essay II discusses this Holy Spirit baptism in detail. It is the initial gift and heart transformation of the Holy Spirit when a person repents and confesses Jesus as savior and Lord. This initial work of the Holy Spirit is called different names in different Scriptures including *baptized, receiving,* and *sealed.* What could be confusing is how the initial Presence of the Holy Spirit in a believer's heart is manifested. Sometimes it is with supernatural tongues; sometimes it is not. Sometimes there is great emotion; sometimes it is a quiet experience as has been discussed earlier. The point is that all believers experience this Holy Spirit baptism at the moment of salvation, as Paul reveals. It happens only one time in the believer's life.

The second ministry of the Holy Spirit in I Corinthians 12:13 is, "and were all made to drink of one Spirit." Notice that the word Paul uses to describe this second ministry of the Holy Spirit is not a one-time only event. *Drinking* is an ongoing lifetime process similar to drinking water or any other liquid to sustain life. It is necessary every day. This metaphor for daily experiencing the Holy Spirit's Power and Presence is consistent with what Jesus said to the woman at the well in John 4:14:

> But whoever drinks of the water that I will give him shall never thirst; but the water that I give him will become in him a well of water springing up to eternal life.

Similarly,

> "If anyone is thirsty, let him come to Me and drink. He who believes in Me, as the Scripture said, from his innermost being will flow rivers of living water." But this He spoke of the Spirit, whom those who believed in Him were to receive; for the Spirit was not yet given, because Jesus was not yet glorified. (John 7:37–39)

Paul further expands this drinking metaphor by connecting drinking with being filled with the Holy Spirit. "And do not get drunk with wine, for that is dissipation, but be filled with the Spirit" (Ephesians 5:18). Paul illustrates the process of being filled with the Spirit as analogous to drinking wine. While drinking too much wine is not good, drinking the Holy Spirit to the point of a change in attitude and behavior is good. In the following verses, Paul gives the definitive Scriptural definition of how a believer in Jesus demonstrates the results of being filled with the Holy Spirit:

> Speaking to one another in psalms and hymns and spiritual songs, singing and making melody with your heart to the Lord; always giving thanks for all things in the name of our Lord Jesus Christ to God, even the Father; and be subject to one another in the fear of Christ. (Ephesians 5:19–21)

It is not an accident that this description begins and ends with the phrase *to one another*. The Holy Spirit brings unity and community in the Body of Christ. The Holy Spirit will always bring love and unity among believers, of all types. Love is the fruit of the Holy Spirit (Galatians 5:22–23). A person filled with the Holy Spirit will manifest the behavior that I Corinthians 13 describes.

Paul gives three distinct manifestations of the Holy Spirit in a believer's heart—praise, thanksgiving, and submission—all in the context of community. These three attitudes are consistent with all of Scripture. It takes supernatural power to manifest these attitudes when things are not going our way. Think of Paul and Silas in jail (Acts 16:25), Corrie Ten Boom in a German concentration camp during WW II (2), and Darlene Rose in a Japanese concentration camp during WW II (3). They all bear witness to the Power of the Holy Spirit to bring joy in the midst of suffering. Paul's role in revealing the deeper, more comprehensive meaning of New Testament doctrine is clear when he gives specific attitudes and behaviors that are consistent with being filled with or drinking the Holy Spirit in his letter to the Ephesians. In the book of Acts, other manifestations of the filling are mentioned such as speaking in unknown tongues (Acts 2:4), preaching (Acts 4:8, 31), healing (Acts 9:17), and supernatural judgment (Acts 13:9–12). The Holy Spirit does operate supernaturally in the life of a believer in all these ways and in many other supernatural manifestations. However, Paul gives in Ephesians 5:19–21 the ultimate goal of Holy Spirit power in a believer's heart and life: the supernatural love of Jesus Himself, expressed in the community of believers. As mentioned earlier,

The Wind That Never Changes

love and unity among the company of believers are the only two evidences that will speak to the world. The Holy Spirit has and will continue to use signs and wonders to glorify Jesus. But the greatest evidence of the glory of Jesus is a human being transformed into the image of Christ by the Holy Spirit (II Corinthians 3:18).

Jesus gives another illustration of how being continually filled with the Holy Spirit is in the context of daily partaking.

> Now suppose one of you fathers is asked by his son for a fish; he will not give him a snake instead of a fish, will he? Or if he is asked for an egg, he will not give him an scorpion, will he? If you then, being evil, know how to give good gifts to your children, how much more will your heavenly Father give the Holy Spirit to those who ask Him! (Luke 11:12–13)

Notice that Jesus calls fish and bread "good things." In the illustration, Jesus could have used any number of things a child could ask of a Father such as clothes or some other tangible item necessary for life. Jesus chose food. He chose food because we are to learn that asking for the Holy Spirit is not a once and for all process. He wants us to seek the Presence and power of the Holy Spirit every moment of every day. Essay II pointed out that the story of Israel from Egypt to Canaan was an allegory for the normal Christian life:

> For I do not want you to be unaware, brethren, that our fathers were all under the cloud and all passed through the sea; and all were baptized into Moses in the cloud and in the sea; and all ate the same spiritual food; and all drank the same spiritual drink, for they were drinking from a spiritual rock which followed them; and the rock was Christ. (I Corinthians 10:1–4)

Notice how similar this story of the nation of Israel is to the discussion on being baptized in the Holy Spirit and eating and drinking the Holy Spirit. Israel was first baptized into Moses in the cloud, which represents the Holy Spirit. After coming out of Egypt, the nation was baptized into Moses in the sea. This is the order for a believer, baptized into Christ in the Holy Spirit and in water. After water baptism, Israel ate spiritual bread and spiritual drink for the next forty years as the generation that came out of Egypt died. This is the death of the flesh for a Christian. The generation that grew up in the wilderness eating and drinking spiritually is the new man in Christ growing in grace. So also, the believer eats and drinks the Holy Spirit every day and grows into a mature saint. This life of choosing consciously to live in the Presence of God in the power of the Holy Spirit is consistent in Scripture: "Pray without ceasing" (I Thessalonians 5:17). This does not mean we are to constantly pray every day and do nothing else, but to develop a habit of actively acknowledging and welcoming the power and Lordship of Jesus into every thought and activity. This happens by the Holy Spirit. Another way of saying this is, "Whatever you do in word or deed, do all in the name of the Lord Jesus, giving thanks through Him to God the Father" (Colossians 3:17).

When it comes to partaking and experiencing the Holy Spirit after salvation, the Scriptures teach that it is an ongoing lifetime process similar to drinking and eating every day of our lives. For our natural life, we need drink and food for the body. Natural drink and food are the source of energy the body needs. For our spiritual life, we need to drink and eat the Holy Spirit every day for spiritual energy and health. Jesus said, "Blessed are those who hunger and thirst for righteousness, for they shall be satisfied" (Matthew 5:6). This expresses the Holy-Spirit-motivated desire for more and more of God. Only God satisfies. It should be obvious that the things of this life, of themselves, cannot satisfy the longings of the human heart. Solomon said, "He has also set eternity in their heart" (Ecclesiastes 3:11). Created in the image of God, man has an eternal spirit that cannot be satisfied with anything but God Himself. Money, power, sex, drugs, possessions, and all the other things humans long for and chase ultimately will result in emptiness. It takes the revelation of the Holy Spirit for a human to realize that only Jesus really satisfies. We can enjoy many things in this world but only if they are under the Lordship of Christ and filled with the presence and blessing of God. The moment we start exalting things above God in our heart, idolatry creeps in and the result is emptiness.

Why should a believer hunger and thirst for righteousness? Righteousness is the expression of the very life of Jesus Himself. He is the only human that has ever lived that was righteous. *Righteous* means much more than just being good. Similar to the word *holy*, *righteousness* expresses the perfect balance of all that is glorious about God such as love, mercy, grace, faithfulness, patience, kindness, justice, beauty, power, etc. Paul tells us that our rightful inheritance as believers is "righteousness, peace, and joy in the Holy Spirit" (Romans 14:17). The order is important. First is the imputed righteousness of Christ as a gift, when we receive Jesus as savior and Lord (II Corinthians 5:21). The righteousness of Christ brings us into peace with God (Romans 5:1), which is the foundation for all peace in the human heart. Finally, peace with God brings the joy of His salvation to every aspect of our being as His life is expressed in us. The Holy Spirit accomplishes all this. Nothing in the world system can give a human these three gifts that are available only in Jesus. Hungering and thirsting for righteousness is desiring more of Jesus to pervade, prompt, and govern in our heart for His glory and kingdom.

Similar to hunger and thirst for food and drink, there are variations in desire. If there has ever been a time in a person's life that they experienced great hunger for food or intense thirst for water, the memory of satisfying that desire is very vivid. So also in hungering and thirsting for righteousness for the life of God as imparted by the Holy Spirit. There are times when God allows circumstances that cause the desire for more of the Holy Spirit to build to a passionate level. When God satisfies that passionate, consuming desire, the results can be equally vivid and life changing. God sometimes overwhelms His children with a supernatural manifestation of Himself that leads to being literally knocked to the floor. The term for this is "being slain in the Spirit," although this phrase is not in the Bible. It is a time when the presence of God is manifested so powerfully that it brings about a literal physical reaction as with Paul in Acts 9:4, the solders sent to arrest Jesus in John 18:6, and the worshiper in I Corinthians 14:25. There are many examples in Christian history of the presence of God causing people to fall to the ground. This is not common in all circumstances, but it is an example of how God sometimes works in our lives.

One last thought on the being filled with the Spirit of Truth. Consider a controversial and hard-to-understand statement of Jesus:

> So Jesus said to them, "Truly, truly, I say to you, unless you eat the flesh of the Son of Man and drink His blood, you have no life in yourselves." (John 6:53)

This is an especially difficult word to a Jew since the Law commanded that a person should never drink blood of any type (Leviticus 3:17). Yet, Jesus says, "Truly, truly," which means He is giving special emphasis to this statement.

> Does this cause you to stumble? What then if you see the Son of Man ascending to where He was before? *It is the Spirit who gives life*; the flesh profits nothing; the words that I have spoken to you are spirit and are life. (John 6:61–63; emphasis added)

Clearly, Jesus is not talking about literal flesh and blood because He said, "the flesh profits nothing." He is telling us in the last half of John 6 that the Holy Spirit imparts to us the eternal life of Jesus as we eat and drink the Holy Spirit. Jesus defines what this means: "I am the bread of life; he who comes to me will not hunger, and he who believes in Me will never thirst" (John 6:35). *Eating the flesh of Jesus is coming to Him, and drinking the blood of Jesus is believing in Him.* This is a supernatural mystery. The Holy Spirit imparts to us the life of Jesus as we come to Jesus and believe in Jesus for all our fears, needs, wants, and anything else (I Peter 1:8). In doing this on a day-by-day basis we find He is all we need. His mercy and grace is sufficient. Jesus is enough. He emphasizes the supernatural nature of this process when He says, "What then if you see the Son of Man ascending to where He was before?" (John 6:62). Jesus is saying that He just told them something mildly spiritual. How could they, and we deal with a real spiritual revelation like seeing Him in heaven? Jesus makes a similar statement to Nicodemus in John chapter 3 when discussing what it means to be "born again." When Nicodemus questions how a person could be born again, Jesus answers, "If I told you earthly things and you do not believe, how can I tell you heavenly things? No one has ascended into heaven, but He who descended from heaven: the Son of Man" (John 3:12–13). Here again, similar to the discussion in John 6, Jesus is telling Nicodemus something that can only be understood in a spiritual context.

In summary, experiencing the Holy Spirit's filling is an ongoing, daily partaking in the life of a believer like drinking and eating natural food. Partaking of the Holy Spirit always involves asking and receiving by faith:

> Ask, and it shall be given you; seek, and you shall find; knock; and it shall be opened unto you. (Matthew 7:7)

Obedience is also a factor. Obedience to the commandments of God are defined by this verse:

> This is His commandment, that we believe in the name of His Son Jesus Christ, and love one another just as He commanded us. (I John 3:23)

This verse sums up all of New Testament theology regarding our relationship to God and each other. The name Jesus means "Jehovah is Salvation." Believing in His name means we believe and receive by faith that Jesus Himself is the provision for all our needs and wants. This is not trivial. It reality it can only be done in the power of the Holy Spirit. Entering into the fullness of believing in the name of Jesus leads to perfect rest (Hebrews 4:10–11). For a believer, the first and greatest commandment is to believe in the Name of Jesus for everything. The second commandment covers our relationships with each other: "A new commandment I give to you, that you love one another even as I have loved you, that you also love one another" (John 13:34). This supersedes the Old Testament commandment of loving our neighbor as our self. We have the supernatural love of God because of the Holy Spirit. We can love each other as God loves in the power of the Holy Spirit. Living by faith and obedience to the commandments of God aligns our heart with the heart of God. To the degree we allow the Holy Spirit to bring us into fullness of faith and obedience, eternal life will be manifested in our earthly existence. God's kingdom is about bringing Heaven to earth in his children.

When we by faith ask our Father for the Holy Spirit, it is up to Him how He wants the Holy Spirit to fill us. It can vary from a quiet moment of strength and encouragement when we need it to an out of body experience in which the Spirit transports us up to heaven or somewhere else (II Corinthians 12:3-4). Many times the Holy Spirit will give us a special filling or anointing for a specific task. In all cases, the Holy Spirit's actions in a believer are consistent with the Word of God and glorifying Jesus and advancing His kingdom. The overarching principles are always the love of Jesus and unity in the body of Christ.

> And He gave some as apostles, and some as prophets, and some as evangelists, and some as pastors and teachers, for the equipping of the saints for the work of service, to the building up of the body of Christ: until we all attain to the unity of the faith, and of the knowledge of the Son of God, to a mature man, to the measure of the stature which belongs to the fullness of Christ. But speaking the truth in love, we are to grow up in all aspects unto Him who is the head, even Christ. (Ephesians 4:11–13, 15)

Sevenfold Ministry of the Holy Spirit to the Believer

Truth

The first ministry of the Holy Spirit is truth. Jesus said,

> But when He, the Spirit of truth, comes, He will guide you into all the truth; for He will not speak on His own initiative, but whatever He hears, He will speak; and He will disclose to you what is to come. (John 16:13)

Jesus said "I am the truth" (John 14:6). Speaking of believers, Jesus also said, "Sanctify them in the truth; Your word is truth" (John 17:17). This applies to the living Word, Jesus; the written word, the scriptures; and the supernatural word as revealed to each believer by the Holy Spirit. The supernatural word is in perfect harmony with the living Word and the written Word.

As an example of how this works, consider conviction of sin by the Holy Spirit. The written word says, "All have sinned and fall short of the glory of God" (Romans 3:23). This is truth as revealed by God. However, this truth fails to impact and change the human heart if it is just received intellectually. The Holy Spirit takes the written Word and makes it truth by revelation to the human heart. This is the supernatural Word. The Holy Spirit penetrates the human heart with the written Word. It is beyond understanding. It is in the spirit of man. It brings about a deep spiritual transformation that leads to conviction, repentance, and receiving Jesus as Savior and Lord. Therefore, the written Word becomes transforming Truth by the Holy Spirit that leads to repentance and faith in the living Word, Jesus. All progress in the Christian life comes this way.

The truth of God's word becomes real and transformative to the heart and spirit of the believer by the Holy Spirit.

> As for you, the anointing which you received from Him abides in you, and you have no need for anyone to teach you; but as His anointing teaches you about all things, and is true and not a lie, and just as it has taught you, you abide in Him. (I John 2:27)

The anointing is the Holy Spirit. He is the Teacher for the believer. This does not mean that we should not listen and learn from gifted teachers that are a gift from the Father to the Church. The point is that we cannot really learn and be transformed by what we hear either from the scriptures or from someone teaching without the revelation of the Holy Spirit. Millions of people hear the truth every day but they are not brought to repentance and salvation. Unless the Holy Spirit penetrates the heart and spirit of the person listening, hearing the Truth intellectually is shallow and powerless.

A good example of this is in the book of Acts. Paul was preaching Truth about Jesus to women by a river:

> A woman named Lydia, from the city of Thyatria, a seller of purple fabrics, a worshiper of God, was listening; and the Lord opened her heart to respond to the things spoken by Paul. (Acts, 16:14)

Paul was preaching the Truth. Lydia was listening to the Truth. The Truth did not do Lydia any good until the Holy Spirit opened her heart leading to a response of repentance and belief in Jesus. This is the supernatural Word penetrating the heart.

The supernatural Word from the Holy Spirit comes to believers in Jesus all the time. Unfortunately, many believers are not taught that this is the normal Christian life: a living, dynamic relationship with an infinite God. The Holy Spirit makes the scriptures real, relevant and life changing. The Bible is an exciting book if we let the Holy Spirit teach us. The Holy Spirit also speaks and reveals to the believer regarding things hidden, like how to pray for others, problems in the spiritual realm that are unknown by the senses, demonic strongholds that can be brought down by prayer and faith, insight into hearts that only God knows, specific instructions on what He wants us to do like witness to someone or pray for someone, or sometimes just telling us that He loves us and is with us. Everything the Holy Spirit reveals to our heart and spirit about Jesus the Truth is to bring us more and more into our inheritance of "righteousness, peace, and joy in the Holy Spirit" (Romans 14:17). This is the eternal life of Jesus manifested in our life. This is the goal of revealed Truth. By the mercy and grace of God in Christ, we can walk in eternal life now.

Faith

> For through the grace given to me I say to everyone among you not to think more highly of himself than he ought to think; but to think so as to have sound judgment, as God has allotted to each a measure of faith. (Romans 12:3)

God has given an amount of faith to each believer in Jesus

The Wind That Never Changes

Christ. The Holy Spirit gives that faith (I Corinthians 12:9). The faith given by the Holy Spirit is a gift from God (Ephesians 2:8). Like any gift, how is it used? Faith is a gift that motivates action (James 2:26). Suppose a person is required to dig a large hole in the ground. At first, all the person has is their hands. Then someone comes up and gives them a shovel as a gift. They receive the shovel and keep digging with their hands. The gift of the shovel does not help when it comes to digging the hole unless they use it. It is the same way with faith from the Holy Spirit.

Another example: Suppose someone promises a large sum of money as a gift to be given in exactly a week. If that person is truthful and has the capability to give such a large amount of money away, what is the response? One response is a wait and see attitude. This is not faith. A second response is that the money is as good as the promise. How good is the promise? If it is a good promise, then there is cause for excited anticipation and action that accompanies receiving a large sum of money. Excited anticipation and action is an expression of faith that results in action. Even though the money has not been delivered yet, confidence in the promise produces joyful anticipation and conviction that the money will surely be delivered as promised: "Now faith is the assurance of things hoped for, the conviction of things not seen" (Hebrews 11:1).

The Christian life is based on faith:

> And without faith it is impossible to please Him, for he who comes to God must believe that He is and that He is a rewarder of those who seek Him. (Hebrews 11:6)

> For I am not ashamed of the gospel, for it is the power of God for salvation to everyone who believes, to the Jew first and also to the Greek. For in it the righteousness of God is revealed from faith to faith; as it is written, "But the righteous man shall live by faith." (Romans 1: 16–17)

Since faith is essential for the Christian life, how is faith imparted to the human spirit by the Holy Spirit? The process begins with the initial step of salvation. The Holy Spirit uses the Word of God to penetrate the human spirit with Truth as previously discussed. With this revelation of the Truth about Jesus comes conviction of sin and belief in Jesus for salvation. At this point, the Holy Spirit is imparting faith for salvation to the repentant sinner (Ephesians 2:8). After receiving Jesus by faith for salvation, the Holy Spirit takes up permanent residence in the spirit of man (Ephesians 1:13–14). Because the spirit of man was dead prior to salvation in Jesus, "the law of sin and of death" reigned in the heart of man (Romans 8:2). This is true for everyone who has not received Jesus as savior (Ephesians 2:1). Human nature has no power against the law of sin and of death. The default mode of human nature without salvation in Jesus is enmity against God, servitude to the spiritually dead human spirit, and powerless exposure to demonic spiritual influence. A careful study of scripture will confirm this tragic condition without Christ.

It is a common belief and practice among followers of all religions that bad behavior can be overcome if one works really hard to be good (whatever *good* means). Consider for a moment the law of gravity. Suppose a person holds an arm straight out from his body horizontal to the ground and is told he must hold it there for the rest of his life to please God. No matter how determined the person is to hold his arm straight out, gravity will always win. Gravity wins because it is a law. Human effort to overcome a spiritual law will never work. The law of sin and of death always wins (Colossians 2:23). The gift of the Holy Spirit to indwell the spirit of a believer in Jesus brings a new law into operation in the human heart: "Therefore there is now no condemnation for those who are in Christ Jesus. For the law of the Spirit of life in Christ Jesus has set you free from the law of sin and of death" (Romans 8:1–2). The process of growth in the Christian life is the progressive expression of "the law of the Spirit of life in Christ Jesus" in the human heart. This is the very life of Jesus Himself indwelling the spirit of a believer in the Presence of the Holy Spirit. Before salvation in Jesus, a person has no power against the law of sin and of death and is a slave to this law. No human effort, no matter how sincere, can break

The Wind That Never Changes

the chains of this bondage. The power of God as expressed in His salvation sets one free from the law of sin and of death. His salvation is a Person, Jesus Christ.

Before salvation in Jesus, a human being has one powerful influence on his heart: the law of sin and of death. This explains the tragedy of human history. The primary characteristic of the law of sin and of death is self-centeredness. Life is all about what I want and me. The primary characteristic of the law of the Spirit of life is Jesus-centeredness. It is all about Jesus and His kingdom. After salvation in Jesus, the believer has a second, more powerful influence on his heart: the law of the Spirit of life. The believer in Jesus has a choice for the first time in his or her life.

> Do not be deceived, God is not mocked; for whatever a man sows, this he will also reap. For the one who sows to his own flesh [the law of sin and of death] will from the flesh reap corruption, but the one who sows to the Spirit [the law of the Spirit of life] will from the Spirit reap eternal life. (Galatians 6: 7–8)

Believers in Jesus have moment-by-moment choices for the rest of their life: submission to the flesh or the Holy Spirit. If a person, even as a born again believer in Jesus, consistently choses to act on the promptings of the flesh, they will experience sadness and emptiness—death, not life. God does not want it this way in His children. He has given His children His Spirit to help them make the good choices that please Him and bring eternal life to them. He has also given His children His Word to build faith: "So faith comes by hearing, and hearing by the word of Christ" (Romans 10:17).

His intention is that His children experience eternal life while still on the earth. Eternal life is the righteousness, peace, and joy of Jesus in us, the hope of glory. Moment by moment every person experiences choices between the flesh and the Holy Spirit. Is this selfish, negative, or critical thought embellished or dismissed? Is a desire for self-pity entertained or given to Jesus? These types of thoughts, and all the similar thoughts, attitudes, and actions of the flesh, which constantly present themselves, have to be put to death.

> For the mind set on the flesh is death, but the mind set on the Spirit is life and peace. (Romans 8:6)
>
> For if you are living according to the flesh, you must die; but if by the Spirit you are putting to death the deeds of the body, you will live. (Romans 8:13)
>
> Then Jesus said to his disciples, "If anyone wishes to come after Me, he must deny himself and take up his cross and follow Me." (Matthew 16:24)

Denying oneself is not giving into the desires of the mind and flesh. Taking up the cross of Jesus means recognizing and receiving by faith that our old man, the flesh, died with Jesus on the cross and no longer has any power over us. By faith imparted by the Word of God and the indwelling Holy Spirit, we see those sinful thoughts, attitudes, and actions as dead because they died with Jesus on the cross and we leave them there. We renounce all hidden things of darkness that come up in our heart.

> So then, my beloved, just as you have always obeyed, not as in my presence only, but now much more in my absence, work out your own salvation with fear and trembling, for it is God who is at work in you, both to will and to work for His good pleasure. (Philippians 2:12-13)

God the Holy Spirit is in the heart of every believer in Jesus to provide the desire and the power to do the will of the Father. Without the Holy Spirit, there would be no battle.

> But I say, walk by the Spirit, and you will not carry out the desire of the flesh. For the flesh sets its desire against the Spirit, and the Spirit against the flesh; for these are in opposition to one another, so that you may not do the things that you please. But if you are led by the Spirit, you are not under the Law. (Galatians 5:17-18)
>
> For all who are being led by the Spirit of God, these are sons of God. For you have not received a spirit of slavery leading to fear again, but you have received a spirit of adoption as sons by which we cry out, "Abba! Father!" (Romans 8:14-15)
>
> But we all, with unveiled face, beholding as in a mirror the glory of the Lord, are being transformed into the same image from glory to glory, just as from the Lord, the Spirit. (II Corinthians 3:18)

After salvation in Jesus, the purpose of God for each believer is being transformed into the image of Christ by the Holy Spirit. It is a process. In the scriptures, it is called growing up, sanctification, discipleship, becoming a father in the faith, being spiritual, maturity, full grown, etc. It means becoming what God intended for His children, manifesting the life of Jesus by showing forth His glory (Exodus 34:6–7) and the fruit of the Spirit (Galatians 5:22–23). Faith in the character and promises of God are central to this process. The indwelling Holy Spirit imparts the required faith to the human heart. However, it is always a choice for the believer to exercise that faith by choosing God's will instead of his own will. It is not supposed to be easy. It requires death to self. The best example of this is Jesus. In the garden just before His arrest, Jesus prayed: "And He went a little beyond them, and fell on His face and prayed, saying, 'My Father, if it is possible, let this cup pass from Me; yet not as I will, but as You will'" (Matthew 26:39). Jesus, as perfect God and perfect man, had to make a choice and submit His will to His Father's will. This is the Christian life. The indwelling Holy Spirit gives the faith to make those hard choices for the glory of God.

Love

> The love of God has been poured out within our hearts through the Holy Spirit who was given to us. (Romans 5:5)

The implications of this verse are profound. "God is love" (I John 4:8). The fundamental character of God is love. He defines and manifests love by His nature. Love governs all His attitudes and actions. He is the Source of all love in time and eternity. Perfect love defines the relationships in the Godhead: Father, Son, and Holy Spirit.

> The Father loves the son. (John 3:35)

> So that the world may know that I love the Father, I do exactly as the Father commanded Me. (John 14:31)

> The love of the Spirit. (Romans 15:30)

For all eternity, the family relationship between the Father, Son, and Holy Spirit has been perfect love. "Beyond all these things put on love, which is the perfect bond of unity" (Colossians 3:14). Perfect love and unity in the Godhead is characterized by perfect righteousness, peace and joy.

When God created man, there was agreement in the Godhead.

> Then God said, "Let Us make man in Our image, according to Our likeness." (Genesis 1:26)

Creation was an action of all three of the Godhead.

> God created man in His own image, in the image of God He created him; male and female He created them. (Genesis 1:27)

A unique aspect of man when compared to all other animals is his spirit. Animals have a body and soul (Genesis 1:30). Man has a body, soul, and spirit (I Thessalonians 5:23). The spirit of man makes him unique in all creation. The unique aspect of man that represents the image of God is an eternal spirit. Man alone has the capacity to have a relationship with God because God created him with a spirit.

Adam and Eve had a spiritual relationship with God before they sinned (Genesis 2:15). After sin entered the human race, the spirit of man was dead and incapable of communing with God (Genesis 3:24; Ephesians 2:1). God told Adam he would die if he ate of the tree of the knowledge of good and evil (Genesis 2:17). God meant a spiritual death, not a physical death. After Adam and Eve sinned and their spirits died, God promised to provide a remedy that would restore spiritual life to the human race (Genesis 3:15). That remedy is Jesus Christ, God Himself (John 3:16). God has provided Himself as the necessary sacrifice for sin so that man can become spiritually alive again (Ephesians 2:5–6).

However, God gives us much more in Christ than we lost in Adam (Romans 5:10, 15, 17). A significant aspect of the much more in Christ is that God has adopted us into His family (Ephesians 1:5):

> Because you are sons, God has sent forth the Spirit of His Son into our hearts, crying, "Abba! Father!" (Galatians 4:6)

Jesus has given believers in Him His glory:

> The glory which You have given Me I have given to them, that they may be perfected in unity, so that the world may know that You sent Me, and loved them, even as you have loved Me. (John 17:22-23)

Mercy, grace, patience, lovingkindness, truth, faithfulness, and holiness are the seven characteristics of the glory of God (Exodus 34:6-7). These seven characteristics are unique to God. His love is the motivating factor in expressing His glory. Since the literal love of God has been poured out in the heart of a believer, the glory of God can be and should be expressed in the heart and life of a believer. Notice that Jesus gave us His glory so we could be perfected in unity. Mercy is forgiveness. Believers have supernatural capacity for forgiveness in the power of the Holy Spirit. Believers in Jesus have all the manifestations of the glory of God because of the indwelling Holy Spirit. God has given believers in Jesus His very nature: "Christ in you, the hope of glory" (Colossians 1:27). The perfect love of God is expressing the glory of God in the heart and life of a believer in Jesus. This is the supernatural ministry of love in the believer's heart by the Holy Spirit. God the Father has taken the Body of Christ into the very heart of the Godhead. The Father loves believers in Jesus the same way He loves Jesus. Believers in Jesus can love the Father the same way Jesus loves the Father because of the indwelling Holy Spirit. Believers in Jesus can love others and manifest the glory of God in the same way that God loves others because of the indwelling Holy Spirit. This is not religion. This is the manifestation of eternal life on earth. This is the life of love: "Christ, who is our life" (Colossians 3:4).

Glory

> The glory which You have given Me I have given to them, that they may be

one, just as We are one. (John 17:22)

In this verse, Jesus is speaking of each member of His body, the church. He is letting each member of His body know that He has given every believer His glory. It is part of salvation in Jesus and imparted to each member by the Holy Spirit. The reason each member needs the glory of Jesus is so the members of His body can be one, even as Jesus and His Father are one. This is another stunning revelation. It is God's intention that human beings enter into a oneness with each other that mirrors the unity in the Godhead. On the human level this is impossible due to the inherent selfish it-is-all-about-me attitude of the flesh.

In Exodus chapters 25 through 31, Moses was on Mount Sinai for forty days receiving instructions from God and the Ten Commandments. The people got impatient and decided to make their own god, a golden calf. Then they had the audacity to proclaim, "This is your god, O Israel, who brought you up from the land of Egypt" (Exodus 32:4). Not only did they make a molten idol in disobedience to God's commandment, they gave the idol credit for delivering them from slavery in Egypt! While this sounds ludicrous, in principle the same thing happens today. Unbelievers in Jesus do not give God credit for what possessions, happiness, or satisfaction they may enjoy in life, but give credit to created things like their own abilities or fortunate events in life that brought success. They are completely ignorant that God "Himself gives to all people life and breath and all things" (Acts 17:25): life at conception, breath at birth, and everything else for the rest of their lives. Even believers in Jesus can fall into this trap because of pride. "For from Him and through Him and to Him are all things. To Him be the glory forever. Amen" (Romans 11:36). All things are of God. Humans can take credit for nothing.

Moses was so exasperated with the nation of Israel that he made a special request from God. He knew that leading this nation for God was not going to be an easy task. He realized that he needed to know God better.

> Now therefore, I pray You, if I have found favor in Your sight, let me know Your ways that I may know You, so that I may find favor in Your sight. Consider too, that this nation is Your people.(Exodus 33:13)
>
> Then Moses said, "I pray You, show me Your glory!" (Exodus 33:18)

God agreed to show Moses His glory and instructed him to be on Mount Sinai early the next morning.

> The next morning The LORD descended in the cloud and stood there with him as he called upon the name of the LORD. Then the LORD passed by in front of him and proclaimed, "The LORD, the LORD God, compassionate and gracious, slow to anger, and abounding in lovingkindness and truth; who keeps lovingkindness for thousands, who forgives iniquity, transgression and sin; yet He will by no means leave the guilty unpunished, visiting the iniquity of fathers on the children and on the grandchildren to the third and fourth generations." (Exodus 34:5–7)

In showing Moses His glory, God revealed seven aspects of His character: mercy, grace, patience, lovingkindness, truth, faithfulness, justice. Notice the order. Mercy is first and justice is last. God is showing Moses His nature. God is showing Moses His response to the sinful, rebellious nature of man. He loves humanity and wants to forgive them and bless them. He greatly desires that man will repent and submit to Him so he can heal them and bless them. He does not want to judge them and punish them but His holy nature demands that He will.

> Say to them, "As I live!" declares the LORD God, "I take no pleasure in the death of the wicked, but rather that the wicked turn from his way and live. Turn back, turn back from your evil ways! Why then will you die, O house of Israel?" (Ezekiel 33:11)

These seven attributes, mercy, grace, patience, lovingkindness, truth, faithfulness, justice, are the glory of God. Who can forgive sin but God? Who can give anything to anyone but God? Who but God is the perfect manifestation of the rest of these attributes? No created being can inherently manifest these attributes. They come solely from God alone. He alone is worthy of glory. His glory is the antidote to the ignorant, rebellious nature of man who always wants to be his own god. This is as ludicrous as the nation of Israel giving the golden calf credit for delivering them from slavery in Egypt.

> But God demonstrates His own love toward us, in that while we were yet sinners, Christ died for us. Much more then, having now been justified by His blood, we shall be saved from the wrath of God through Him. For if while we were enemies we were reconciled to God through the death of His Son, much more, having been reconciled, we shall be saved by His life. (Romans 5:8–10)

Jesus Christ was the perfect manifestation of the glory of God in human form. His obedience to the Father in His death, burial, and resurrection made the glory of God available to all those who repent and believe the gospel. Notice in the verses above, "we were reconciled to God through the death of His son": this is salvation. "We shall be saved by His life": this is sanctification. Christ in you, the hope of glory (Colossians 1:27).

By the Holy Spirit, Jesus has given each member of His body His glory. How does this supernatural glory work in the life of a believer? If the glory of God is given to believers to develop unity, what kinds of things inhibit unity? Probably one that leads the list is unforgiveness. Believers in Jesus are still human. Anyone who gets really close to another human being will quickly see flaws in that human. No one "has it together." Only Jesus "had it together," and walked in perfection before the Father. The rest of humanity fails regularly: "For we all stumble in many ways" (James 3:2). Because of human frailty, there will always be a need for forgiveness. It is interesting to note that forgiveness is not optional in the sight of God. Not forgiving from the heart is one of only two sins mentioned in the Scriptures that bring a specific consequence:

> Then summoning him, his lord said to him, "You wicked slave, I forgave you all that debt because you pleaded with me. Should you not also have had mercy on your fellow slave, in the same way that I had mercy on you?" And his lord, moved with anger, handed him over to the torturers until he should repay all that was owed him. My heavenly Father will also do the same to you, if each of you does not forgive his brother from your heart. (Matthew 18:32–35)

The Wind That Never Changes

In this passage, not forgiving opens up the heart to demonic oppression. God allows these torturers because we refuse to forgive. It is clear in the scriptures that certain types of disobedience lead to demonic oppression. This is one of them. Unforgiveness does far more damage to the person who needs to forgive than the person who needs the forgiveness:

> For if you forgive others for their transgressions, your heavenly Father will also forgive you. But if you do not forgive others, then your Father will not forgive your transgressions. (Matthew 6:14–15)

Is a person's will and pride so important that they will sacrifice their fellowship with God to hold on to their unforgiveness? Notice, it is our fellowship with God that is hindered by unforgiveness, not our relationship: "If I regard wickedness in my heart, the Lord will not hear" (Psalm 66:18). If a person is truly born again by the Spirit of God, unforgiveness does not cause one to lose their salvation, but it does hinder our fellowship with God and give Satan an opportunity to attack us:

> But one whom you forgive anything, I forgive also; for indeed what I have forgiven, if I have forgiven anything, I did it for your sakes in the presence of Christ, so that no advantage would be taken of us by Satan, for we are not ignorant of his schemes. (II Corinthians 2:10–11)

So how does the glory of God as provided by the Holy Spirit function in forgiveness? An illustration from the life of Corrie Ten Boom will make it clear (4). After the war, Corrie traveled all over the world testifying about the grace of God—how His grace enabled her to endure years of suffering and loss in Nazi concentration camps during World War II. After one of her talks, a man walked up to meet her. Corrie recognized the man as a savagely cruel guard in one of the concentration camps. He was the guard that killed her sister Betsy. The man had become a Christian after the war and had come to ask Corrie's forgiveness. As Corrie stood there looking at this man, all his cruelty flooded her thoughts and emotions, especially how he beat her sister Betsy to death when she was too weak to work. Corrie told the Lord in her heart, "I can't forgive him, Lord." The Lord spoke to her heart and told her to take his outstretched hand. In obedience to the Lord, Corrie reached out and took the man's hand. At that instant, the love of God flooded her heart and banished all the hatred and unforgiveness she had for this man. She loved him. She really loved him. It was the supernatural love of God in her. She completely forgave the man from her heart. If we submit in obedience to God, the Holy Spirit will enable us to forgive.

It is not always as dramatic as with Corrie. Sometimes we must choose to forgive in our heart. If the issue keeps coming up in our heart, we keep on forgiving. The right emotion will eventually be in our heart if we persevere. Sometimes it takes this approach. It also helps to "put feet on our forgiveness" by seeking to bless the person we are forgiving.

Another very powerful illustration of the glory of God!

> For this finds favor, if for the sake of conscience toward God a person bears up under sorrows when suffering unjustly. For what credit is there if, when you sin and are harshly treated, you endure it with patience.
>
> But if when you do what is right and suffer for it you patiently endure it, this finds favor with God. For you have been called for this purpose, since Christ also suffered for you, leaving you an example for you to follow in His steps, who committed no sin, nor was any deceit found in His mouth; and while being reviled, He did not revile in return; while suffering, He uttered no threats, but kept entrusting Himself to Him who judges righteously. (I Peter 2:19–23)

There are three important points in this passage. First, the word *favor* is the same Greek word translated *grace* elsewhere in the Scriptures. It could correctly be read, "for this finds grace" and "this finds grace with God." Second, the Holy Spirit is revealing in this passage that the followers of Jesus are to be vessels of His grace, "called for this purpose." God will allow us to be in situations in which we are doing the right thing but are suffering because of other people. They may not understand what we are doing or why. Our behavior may not line up with their expectations or theology. Alternatively, they may be spiritually

The Wind That Never Changes

wounded and need an extra portion of God's redemptive love. Very often, a believer in Jesus is called to get involved with a problem they did not cause:

> Those who hate me without a cause are more the hairs of my head; Those who would destroy me are powerful, being wrongfully my enemies; What I did not steal, I then have to restore. (Psalm 69:4)

This is a verse about Jesus. In His passion, death, burial, and resurrection, He restored what was lost in Adam. He was and is the perfect example of being an instrument of grace in suffering. As the passage in Peter above says, "leaving you an example for you to follow in His steps." The Holy Spirit will enable the believer to be an instrument of the grace of God in circumstances that would evoke anger, resentment, outrage, self-pity, judgment, criticism, and a host of other negative emotions.

The call of Jesus to walk with Him is a call to die to one's self. It is a call to learn to walk in redemptive love. That is, to allow the supernatural love and glory of God expression in our attitude, actions, and words so that others will experience Him. This involves a choice on our part. The Holy Spirit desires and is willing to express Himself in us. We can choose to align our heart with the Holy Spirit or align our heart with the flesh. Even the desire to choose is from the Holy Spirit. That is why He is called the Helper:

> When the Helper comes, whom I will send to you from the Father, that is the Spirit of truth who proceeds from the Father, He will testify about Me. (John 15:26)

Our life is to be an expression of the character and nature of God seen by all men. This is what it means to be a follower of Jesus. Jesus invites us to participate in His suffering for the lost, the hurt, the wounded, the sick, etc. Sin has wrought such damage to human hearts. Jesus came to deliver humanity from the power of sin and the devil. He calls us to the same task. As we get closer and closer to Jesus, we will find His burden for the lost to become our burden, His desire to love the unlovely our desire, His ability to see beauty in ashes our ability. Sometimes

He will even bring us to weeping for the lost and those suffering the consequences of their own sinfulness. He allows us to enter into His pain for them:

> Now I rejoice in my sufferings for your sake, and in my flesh I do my share on behalf of His body, which is the church, in filling up what is lacking in Christ's afflictions. (Colossians 1:24)

Are we willing to be a vessel of mercy and grace to a lost and dying world even if it means we suffer for it? This is the heart of God.

Are we are willing to give up our rights for others as Paul instructs?

> Do nothing from selfishness or empty conceit, but with humility of mind regard one another as more important that yourselves; do not merely look out for your own personal interests, but also for the interests of others. (Philippians 2:3–4)

If we do not concern ourselves with our own rights, who will? This is the beautiful, amazing part. As we are willing to submit to the Holy Spirit to be an instrument of grace, the Father takes care of our rights. Jesus gave us the perfect example. This is the third important point in I Peter 2:19–23: "He did not revile in return; while suffering, He uttered no threats, but kept entrusting Himself to Him who judges righteously." Only God can judge righteously because He can see everything in the physical and spiritual realms—past, present and future. Who is better to take care of our rights, us or God? If a person insists on stubbornly taking care of their own rights instead of allowing God to take care of their rights, God will allow them to reap the consequences of their own choices.

This does not mean that followers of Jesus become doormats for everyone to walk over all the time. However, it does mean that God commands us to trust and obey Him when He is telling us to forgive and be gracious in a circumstance that would be impossible in our own strength:

> But we have this treasure in earthen vessels, so that the surpassing greatness of the power will be of God and not from ourselves (II Corinthians

4:7).

If we humble ourselves and ask God for the power to forgive and be gracious in an impossible situation, He will answer our prayer and provide the supernatural power. When we need mercy, grace, patience, lovingkindness, truth, faithfulness, and holiness, God will give them to us for His glory and kingdom. Unity in the Church requires these seven attributes of the glory of God in each believer. The Holy Spirit will do this if we let Him.

Power

> But you will receive power when the Holy Spirit comes upon you; and you shall be my witnesses both in Jerusalem, and all Judea and Samaria, and even to the remotest part of the earth. (Acts 1:8)

> Once God has spoken; twice I have heard this: That power belongs to God. (Psalm 62:11)

There are three unique manifestations of the life of God imparted to the human spirit by the Holy Spirit; love, glory, and power. Glory and the fruit of the Spirit, which is summed up in love, have been discussed previously. Power is the third and final attribute that is unique to God. God is the Source of all love, glory, and power in all creation, both natural and supernatural. God's Love is revealed by I Corinthians 13 and Galatians 5:22-23. God's Glory is revealed by Exodus 34:6-7. God's power is revealed by Jeremiah 32:17:

> Ah Lord God! Behold, You have made the heavens and the earth by Your great power and by your outstretched arm! Nothing is too difficult for You. (Jeremiah 32:17)

Notice the phrase *Nothing is too difficult for You*. "For nothing will be impossible with God" (Luke 1:37). Along with supernatural love and glory, the Holy Spirit gives God's supernatural power to the believer in Jesus:

> For we who live are constantly being delivered over to death for Jesus' sake, so that the life of Jesus also may be manifested in our mortal flesh. (II Corinthians 4:11)

It is natural to think that humans have power or ability to do good. However, "No one is good except God alone" (Luke 18:19). No created being can be good on their own power. God allows trials and difficulties in the life of a believer to bring the believer to humble recognition of their powerless condition when it comes to walking in supernatural power. "Being delivered over to death" is to teach the believers not to trust in themselves but God who gives life to the dead.

> But we have this treasure in earthen vessels, so that the surpassing greatness of the power will be of God and not from ourselves. (II Corinthians 4:7)

God's love, glory, and power are the attributes of the life of Jesus manifested in our mortal flesh. These three attributes have their Source in God, not human flesh. That Source is the Holy Spirit.

Therefore, what does the power of God do in the life of a believer? The power of God enables a believer to be and do good. In the Scriptures, the word *good* always refers to something about God. There is no good apart from God. For a believer to manifest goodness in any way is an expression of the life of Jesus. When the serpent tempted Eve to eat of the tree of the knowledge of good and evil she desired three results: food, delight to the eyes, and wisdom (Genesis 3:6). Compare what Eve saw in the forbidden fruit to what the apostle John says is in the world:

> For all that is in the world, the lust of the flesh and the lust of the eyes and the boastful pride of life, is not from the Father, but is from the world. (I John 2:16)

Notice the three things John says are in the world: lust of the eyes, lust of the flesh, boastful pride of life. Compare these three things to what Eve desired from the forbidden fruit. This is not accidental. The Holy Spirit wrote the Bible from the beginning to end. These three areas express all human sin: lust of the flesh, as in excesses in food, drink, drugs, sex, sloth, etc.; lust of the eyes, as in coveting of all sorts; pride of life, as in superiority for any reason or authority over others. Gratifying the flesh in these ways is all the world of fallen, unregenerate humanity has to offer for happiness. It should be obvious to even the most casual observer that trying to satisfy the flesh is an empty endeavor. Sadly, this is not the case. To this day, the devil has not changed his tactics. He still tempts all humans to sin by suggesting things that will satisfy the flesh, eyes, and pride. Without the Holy Spirit, humans have no power to resist these temptations.

After baptism by John and anointing with the fullness of the Holy Spirit, Jesus was taken by the Spirit into the wilderness to be tempted by the devil (Luke 4:1–2). After Jesus fasted forty days, the devil came to Him with three temptations: tell this stone to become bread, worship me and receive all the kingdoms of the world and their glory, and throw Yourself down from the pinnacle of the temple to demonstrate how important you are (Luke 4:3-13). Compare the order of the three temptations to what Eve desired from the tree and John said was in the world. They are all the same. The very first thing Jesus did after His baptism was to demonstrate His victory over the same three types of temptations that Eve submitted to when she disobeyed God's commandment not to eat of the fruit of the tree. Eve's sin is the sin of the entire human race: "For all have sinned and fall short of the glory of God" (Romans 3:23). Every human being who has ever lived has sinned by yielding to the desires of the flesh, the eyes, and pride. As perfect God and perfect Man, Jesus was victorious over the lust of the flesh, the lust of the eyes, and the pride of life. Jesus is the Righteous One. He never committed a single sin in His entire earthly life:

> For we do not have a high priest who cannot sympathize with our weaknesses, but One who has been tempted in all things as we are, yet without sin. (Hebrews 4:15)

Jesus taking up residence in the spirit and heart of a believer in the Presence of the Holy Spirit means power to overcome temptation. The power is the very life of Jesus Himself:

> For if while we were enemies we were reconciled to God through the death of His Son, much more, having been reconciled, we shall be saved by His life. (Romans 5:10)

Reconciliation saves the believer from the penalty of sin: death. This is salvation. The life of Jesus saves the believer from the dominion of sin, disobedience to God. This is sanctification.

Another aspect of the power of Jesus Himself in the life of a believer is the ability to be a witness for Jesus by living the Gospel and telling others the hope of the Gospel:

> But sanctify Christ as Lord in your hearts, always being ready to make a defense to everyone who asks you to give an account for the hope that is in you, yet with gentleness and reverence. (I Peter 3:15)

If, by the power of Christ in us through the Holy Spirit, we live the gospel, others will see a Christian is different. If others ask why a Christian is different, the Holy Spirit gives the power to testify about Jesus:

> For it is not you who speak, but it is the Spirit of your Father who speaks in you. (Matthew 10:20)

Finally, the Holy Spirit imparts power to the believer to perform signs and wonders such as healing the sick:

> And with great power the apostles were giving testimony to the resurrection of the Lord Jesus, and abundant grace was upon them all. (Acts 4:33)

The apostles were not only speaking divinely inspired words about Jesus; God was also bearing witness to those words by granting supernatural manifestations of Holy Spirit power in healing the sick:

> And my message and my preaching were not in persuasive words of wisdom, but in demonstration of the Spirit and of power, so that your faith would not rest on the wisdom of men, but on the power of God. (I Corinthians 2:4–5)

The power of the Holy Spirit accompanies preaching of the word of God:

> God also testifying with them, both by signs and wonders and by various miracles and by gifts of the Holy Spirit according to His own will. (Hebrews 2:4)

Miraculous signs have accompanied the preaching of the gospel throughout history. Miraculous signs do not always accompany salvation, but they often do accompany salvation. As mentioned earlier, the Holy Spirit manifests His presence and power as He wills.

The third major area of Holy Spirit power in the life of the believer are gifts of the Spirit. Gifts of the Spirit are covered in detail as a separate, later section of this essay. In summary, all power in the life of a believer in Jesus is an expression of the life of Jesus in the believer. Power to overcome sin, witness, and perform supernatural acts is due to the indwelling Christ in the heart of a believer. The Holy Spirit accomplishes all this, and no one can take any credit for this power. It is a gift from God the Father for the glory of Jesus and to advance His kingdom.

> But by His doing you are in Christ Jesus, who became to us wisdom from God, and righteousness and sanctifications, and redemption, so that, just as it is written, "let him who boasts, boast in the Lord." (I Corinthians 1: 30–31)

Authority

> Behold, I give you the authority to trample on serpents and scorpions, and over all the power of the enemy, and nothing shall by any means hurt you. (Luke 10:19)

> For our struggle is not against flesh and blood, but against the rulers, against the powers, against the world forces of this darkness, against the spiritual forces of wickedness in the heavenly places. (Ephesians 6:12)

The Bible teaches that there are unseen but powerful forces of evil in the spirit dimension. This evil, unseen spirit world is a demonic kingdom headed by Satan and has levels of authority (Daniel 10:20). After His resurrection, Jesus took His seat at the right hand of the Father,

> far above all rule and authority and power and dominion, and every name that is named, not only in this age but also in the one to come. And He put

> all things in subjection under His feet, and gave Him as head of all things to the church, which is His body, the fullness of Him who fills all in all. (Ephesians 1:21–23)

Since Jesus personally dwells in every believer, His authority over all evil spirit forces is available to each believer. The practical result of the authority of Jesus in a believer is victory over evil spirit beings such as demons. The Holy Spirit wrote the scriptures in such a way that pulls the veil back a little and allows a glimpse into the spirit world.

We learn most about demonic activity in the four gospels and the book of Acts. Jesus demonstrated complete authority over all the power of spiritual enemies in casting out demons and healing those who had afflictions caused by demons. Demonic activity is also recorded in the Old Testament, Job chapters 1 and 2. Believers in Jesus will sometimes come into contact with demonic oppression, possession, or affliction in another person. It is important to know and understand that Jesus has equipped the believer to discern these situations and deal with them in the authority of the Name of Jesus through the power of the Holy Spirit. Signs that are characteristic of a believer in Jesus are the authority to resist the devil (James 4:7) and cast out demons (Mark 16:17). A good book that covers this subject in detail is *They Shall Expel Demons* by Derek Prince. There are many mysteries in the spirit world, such as generational curses brought on by occult practices. Fascination with evil in the spirit world is forbidden to God's followers (Deuteronomy 18:10–12). Even believers in Jesus either ignorantly or foolishly expose themselves to demonic influence.

> No, but I say that the things which the Gentiles sacrifice, they sacrifice to demons and not to God; and I do not want you to become sharers in demons. (I Corinthians 10:20)

Believers can unknowingly partake of demonic activity by reading books on the occult including witchcraft and other supernatural activity, watching movies based on the occult, or even playing with demon-inspired games. These kinds of things look innocent to the uninformed, but they are not and can lead to demonic oppression. For this reason, the believer in Jesus must be circumspect with regard to what they watch and read.

> Do not participate in the unfruitful deeds of darkness, but instead even expose them; for it is disgraceful even to speak of the things which are done by them in secret. (Ephesians 5:11–12)
>
> Be of sober spirit, be on the alert. Your adversary, the devil, prowls around like a roaring lion, seeking someone to devour. (I Peter 5:8)
>
> ... so that no advantage would be taken of us by Satan, for we are not ignorant of his schemes. (II Corinthians 2:11)

Since these types of demonically-inspired activities are so common and easily available, the believer will often encounter people who need deliverance. The Holy Spirit imparts the discernment and authority to deal with all the powers of evil in the Name of Jesus.

Companionship

> It is not good for the man to be alone. (Genesis 2:18)

From the beginning of creation, God recognized that human beings should not be alone. God created man to need companionship, fellowship, socialization, and, most importantly, emotional support and understanding. People need a relationship with an intelligent being. God created man to have the capability to have relationships with other people and with Himself. After Adam and Eve sinned, that close relationship that existed between God and man in the Garden of Eden was broken. Sin had caused a breach in the relationship between God and man. God made a promise that He would heal that breach and restore a way for man to again be in relationship with God. Jesus did that on the cross, as has been discussed. As is pointed out in the essay on baptism, the cross reaches back to Adam and Eve and reaches forward to the end of time to make complete payment for all sin:

> He Himself is the propitiation for our sins, and not for ours only, but also for those of the whole world. (I John 2:2)

While Jesus paid for the sins of the whole world, past, present, and future, the merits of that payment must be received by faith in His sacrifice. As discussed in Essay I, it is not enough to believe the facts about Jesus; His salvation must be received by faith. Part of His salvation is His promise to always be with those who believe and receive Him:

> I will ask the Father, and He will give you another Helper, that He may be with you forever; that is the Spirit of truth, whom the world cannot receive, because it does not see Him or know Him, but you know Him because He abides with you and will be in you. I will not leave you as orphans; I will come to you. (John 14:16–18)

The Holy Spirit is the eternal Companion of the believer Who dwells in the believer. He brings the presence of Jesus to the spirit and heart of man. God has promised in His Word that He will never leave the believer in Jesus or forsake them (Hebrews 13:5). There are abundant examples in Christian history and the present time where believers in Jesus are tortured or killed for their faith. God gives us His eternal promise that no matter what happens in the life of a believer in Jesus, He will be right there with us, giving us the grace to go through whatever He allows. This is one reason the Holy Spirit is also known as the Comforter.

> For I am convinced that neither death, nor life, nor angels, nor principalities, nor things present, nor things to come, nor powers, nor height, nor depth, nor any other created thing, will be able to separate us from the love of God, which is in Christ Jesus our Lord. (Romans 8:38–39)

Gifts of the Spirit

Gifts of the Holy Spirit given to the believer in Jesus Christ is one of the most controversial subjects in Christianity. The basic question is what gifts of the Holy Spirit are in operation in the present day? Many believe that the so-called supernatural "sign gifts" like speaking in other tongues, divine healing, and prophecy ceased at the end of the Apostolic age around 100 AD. Others believe that these sign gifts, along with all other gifts of the Holy Spirit, are in operation and available to believers in the present age. *Cessationists* teach that the sign gifts ceased. *Continuists* teach that the sign gifts are in operation in the present age. Both groups accept and teach the doctrine that the Holy Spirit gives supernatural gifts to each believer. They only differ in which gifts.

Attitude

It violates the clear commandments of Scripture for either group to judge or criticize the other group:

> Who are you to judge the servant of another? To his own master he stands or falls; and he will stand, for the Lord is able to make him stand. (Romans 14:4)

Unfortunately, judgment and criticism are very common. As the Chinese house churches discussed earlier, instead of showing love and tolerance for one another, cessationists and continuists spend a lot of time and energy judging each other. Christians in general tend to be judgmental and intolerant (I Corinthians 1:12–13). There seems to be an unspoken but strong tendency in each faction to think they are closer to the truth than other groups.

Philippians 2:3–4 gives the biblical attitude that all believers in Jesus Christ should have for other believers.:

> Do nothing from selfishness or empty conceit, but with humility of mind regard one another as more important than yourselves; do not merely look out for your own personal interests, but also for the interest of others.

Even cults and any other religions that do not know or accept the basic doctrines of New Testament Christianity such as the deity of Jesus, His sacrificial death on the cross, and bodily resurrection from the grave merit the love of God (I Timothy 1:15). How can they be reached for Jesus if all they see is judgment and superiority from Christians? It is true that Christians know the Truth and the only way to God the Father (John 14:6). That fact should produce thankfulness, brokenness, and humility. Not pride and superiority:

> Who among you is wise and understanding? Let him show by his good behavior his deeds in the gentleness of wisdom. But if you have bitter jealousy and selfish ambition in your heart, do not be arrogant and lie against the truth. This wisdom is not that which comes down from above, but is earthly, natural, and demonic. For where jealousy and selfish ambition exist, there is disorder and every evil thing. But the wisdom from above is first pure, then peaceable, gentle, reasonable, full of mercy and good fruits, unwavering without hypocrisy. (James 3:13-17)

Even if other believers preach Christ with the wrong motives, Paul gives us a perfect example to follow:

> Some, to be sure, are preaching Christ even from envy and strife, but some also from good will; the latter do it out of love, knowing that I am appointed for the defense of the gospel; the former proclaim Christ out of selfish ambition rather than from pure motives, thinking to cause me distress in my imprisonment. What then? Only that in every way, whether in pretense or in truth, Christ is proclaimed; and in this I rejoice. (Philippians 1:15-18)

Jesus also confirms this loving and tolerant reaction to others who do not walk the way we want or expect them to walk:

> John answered and said, "Master, we saw someone casting out demons in Your name; and we tried to prevent him because he does not follow along with us." But Jesus said to him, "Do not hinder him; for he who is not against you is for you." (Luke 9:49-50)

The divisions and disagreements between believing Christians are usually not due to sinful actions. There are clear directions in Scripture on how to deal with sinful behavior in believing Christians. Mathew chapter 18 and many other passages give instructions on this subject. Divisions and disagreements are usually caused by doctrinal or theological differences of opinions—different ways of interpreting Scripture. These doctrinal or theological differences are rarely central to the Gospel message. There is usually no debate on the central themes of evangelical Christianity. The debates are about issues like traditional or modern music used in worship, doctrines on end time events, what Spiritual gifts are to be practiced in the Church, leadership structure in a local Church,

The Wind That Never Changes

grape juice or wine for communion, and musical instruments used in worship. Such subjects are not foundational to the gospel of Jesus Christ! Yet such secondary issues have divided the Church for centuries. All believers in Jesus should take to heart what Jesus said to the Pharisees:

> But woe to you Pharisees! For you pay tithe of mint and rue and every kind of garden herb, and yet disregard justice and the love of God; but these are the things you should have done without neglecting the others. (Luke 11:42)

As discussed earlier in this essay in the section on "The Foundation of Love," it is so easy to miss or ignore the weightier matters of following Jesus like loving others as He loves us, and major on secondary matters. Loving as Jesus loves requires death to self; the secondary matters do not.

Working of Spiritual Gifts

The first point with regard to spiritual gifts given by the Holy Spirit is that each believer has a spiritual gift:

> But to each one of us grace was given according to the measure of Christ's gift. (Ephesians 4:7)

> As each one has received a special gift, employ it in serving one another as good stewards of the manifold grace of God. (I Peter 4:10)

> But to each one is given the manifestation of the Spirit for the common good. (I Corinthians 12:7)

The second point is how the spiritual gift is to work in the Body of Christ:

> Now there are varieties of gifts, but the same Spirit. And there are varieties of ministries, and the same Lord. There are varieties of effects, but the same God who works all things in all persons. (I Corinthians 12:4–6)

Notice in this passage that 1. the Spirit gives the gift; 2. the Lord Jesus administers the gift; 3. the Father causes the effect of the gift.

> The gifts and calling of God are irrevocable (Romans 11:29).

A believer can have a legitimate spiritual gift from the Holy

Spirit, and yet not use it properly because that believer does not submit to the Lordship of Christ. This is the main cause of confusion and conflict over the supernatural sign gifts. Not submitting to the Lordship of Jesus is a major disconnect in the use of any spiritual gift in the church—especially the sign gifts.

The classic example is the Corinthian church itself. It is clear in Paul's letter and instructions to the Corinthian church, that they had made the gift of tongues a much more important part of worship than the Lord Jesus was leading them to do. The gift of tongues was not practiced in submission to the Lordship and administration of Christ in the Corinthian church. Consequently, this particular gift was not having the effect God intended:

> Therefore if the whole church assembles together and all speak in tongues, and ungifted men or unbelievers enter, will they not say you are mad? (I Corinthians 14:23)

This is just one example of how a sign gift or any gift of the Holy Spirit can be misused if not exercised in prayerful submission to the Lordship of Christ. This practice of everyone in the worship service all speaking in tongues at the same time has continued into the present day in some churches. It is not hard to see how others who do not understand this particular gift have a difficult time accepting it as valid. Paul goes into detail instructing the Corinthian church, and future generations of believers, how to use the gift of tongues in a public worship service. In fact, this is an affirmation by the Holy Spirit that tongues is a gift for all time. Why would the Holy Spirit include in the cannon of Scripture such detailed instructions on how to use gifts like prophecy and tongues if the practice of such gifts were to pass after the apostolic age? I Corinthians chapters 12, 13, and 14 are the most detailed instructions in all of Scripture on spiritual gifts and how to use them. It seems logical that God would include in the cannon of Scripture instructions on how to use the sign gifts for His church that He knew would still need for the next two thousand years. If the sign gifts ceased around 100 AD, why is all this information in the present day Scriptures?

Gift of Apostle

A common reason for the cessation of the sign gifts is the argument that apostolic ministry ceased after John, the last living apostle, died. This argument does not recognize that there are two types of apostles in the New Testament. Jesus Himself personally called the original twelve apostles. This is the primary criterion for the original twelve apostles: Jesus personally called each one. The selection of Matthias to replace Judas as one of the twelve in Acts 1:21-26 does not fit the primary standard for being one of the twelve apostles. This is an example of Peter and the other apostles getting ahead of the Lord in terms of who would replace Judas. Matthias is never mentioned again by name. However, on the road to Damascus, Jesus personally appeared to and called Saul of Tarsus to be an apostle (Acts 9:3-19). In Romans 1:1, I Corinthians 1:1, and I Corinthians 15:9, Paul refers to himself as a called apostle. Paul was the apostle to the gentiles as Peter was the apostle to the Jews (Galatians 2:8). Paul refers to himself as an apostle in all his writings. It should be clear that Paul is the replacement for Judas, and his name will be on one of the foundation stones of the New Jerusalem (Revelation 21:14).

What about Matthias? He could have also been an apostle, but not a called apostle as the original twelve. Matthias could have had the apostolic gift as mentioned in I Corinthians 12:28 and Ephesians 4:11. In I Corinthians 15:3-9 Paul recounts the order of whom Jesus appeared to after His resurrection. First Peter, then to the twelve apostles together, then to five hundred brethren at one time, then to James, then to all the apostles, then to Paul himself. James in this list is not James the brother of John. It is James the brother of Jesus (Galatians 1:19). Therefore, James the Lord's brother was recognized as an apostle as well as another group other than the twelve. In addition, Barnabas is called an apostle in Acts 14:14.

In the order of spiritual gifts, apostle is the greatest gift and prophecy is second (I Corinthians 12:28). A New Testament apostle other than the called twelve is a church planter and leader. Paul referred to James the brother of the Lord, Barnabas, and another group of people as apostles in his writings. While not specifically mentioned, Timothy, Silvanus, and Apollos could have also had the apostolic gift. It should be clear that this group of apostles did not have the same authority and status as the original twelve. To repeat, the gift of apostle is not the same thing as being one of the original twelve apostles personally called by Jesus. When apostleship is brought up in the present day, the argument against apostolic succession is always used as a reason against present day apostles. Present day apostles do not derive their authority from any of the twelve apostles. Present day apostles have the spiritual gift of church planting and leadership on a larger scale than pastors and teachers. Present day apostles do not add to or change the complete cannon of Scripture. As empowered by the Holy Spirit, present day apostles teach, minister and act in complete accord with Scripture.

While present day apostles minister in agreement with Scripture, this does not mean they are perfect. The selection of Matthias makes this point. Peter and the other apostles did not have the leading of the Lord when they close Matthias. This is obvious by what happened later when Jesus chose Paul as the replacement for Judas. Why did the Lord include this in Scripture and make no comment on it? It is there to teach and encourage His children for all time. Mistakes the apostles made are in the Scriptures so we will not be so hard on each other! Consider when Paul had a falling out with Barnabas (Acts 15:36-41) and when Paul called out Peter on his hypocrisy (Galatians 2:11-14). Peter and Paul were chosen apostles but they were also still human! God is not nearly as concerned about the foibles of His children as they are with each other's. No person, no matter how gifted in the Spirit, is going to do everything exactly right! Jesus was the only One who did everything exactly right. All His followers make mistakes. This is why love is foundational. The Holy Spirit put I Corinthians 13 right in the middle of the most controversial subject in the Scriptures, supernatural gifts. Love is most the excellent way, not theological or doctrinal perfection.

Gift of Prophecy

The spiritual gift of apostle is the first and greatest gift. The gift of prophecy is second. The spiritual gift of prophecy is not for all believers, as Paul points out in I Corinthians 12:29. The spiritual gift of prophecy is for delivering special messages from God to His people. These messages are always in harmony with Scripture and do not add to or modify scripture:

> One of them named Agabus stood up and began to indicate by the Spirit that there would certainly be a great famine all over the world. And this took place in the reign of Claudius. (Acts 11:28)

This prophecy was not about the Scriptures in any way. God was simply telling His people of a coming event so they could prepare.

> As we were staying there for some days, a prophet named Agabus came down from Judea. And coming to us, he took Paul's belt and bound his own feet and hands, and said, "This is what the Holy Spirit says: 'In this way the Jews at Jerusalem will bind the man who owns this belt and deliver him into the hands of the Gentiles.'" When we heard this, we as well as the local residents began begging him not to go up to Jerusalem. (Acts 21:10–12)

An important point on this Scripture is how the people interpreted this prophecy. They wrongly concluded that Paul should not to go up to Jerusalem, and tried to persuade him not to go. It is clear from the rest of the book of Acts that Paul was supposed to go up to Jerusalem, be delivered to the Romans, and ultimately appear before Caesar. The Lord appeared to Paul after he was arrested by the Jews and delivered to the Romans:

> But on the night immediately following, the Lord stood at his side and said, "Take courage; for as you have solemnly witnessed to My cause at Jerusalem, so you must witness at Rome also." (Acts 23:11)

As the earlier examples with the Apostles, the early Christians missed things, just as it happens today. Misinterpreting a prophecy is easy to do if human emotion and understanding are allowed to dominate. This is why it is so important to constantly seek the Lord for His wisdom and guidance. Humans are fallible. All prophecy should be spiritually judged.

> Do not quench the Spirit; do not despise prophetic utterances. But examine everything carefully; hold fast to that which is good; abstain from every form of evil. (I Thessalonians 5:19–22)

In addition to foretelling, prophecy is also forth telling specific instructions to believers from the Holy Spirit:

> Now there were at Antioch, in the church that was there, prophets and teachers: Barnabas, and Simeon who was called Niger, and Lucius of Cyrene, and Manaen who had been brought up with Herod the tetrarch, and Saul. While they were ministering to the Lord and fasting, the Holy Spirit said, "Set apart for Me Barnabas and Saul for the work to which I have called them." Then, when they had fasted and prayed and laid their hands on them, they sent them away. (Acts 13: 1–3)

Paul introduces a second aspect of prophecy in I Corinthians chapter 14. While all believers do not have the gift of foretelling and forth telling prophetic ministry, they should aspire to grow and be used of the Holy Spirit in a type of prophecy that is to help others:

> Pursue love, yet desire earnestly that you may prophesy. (I Corinthians 14:1)
>
> For you can all prophesy one by one, so that all may learn and all may be exhorted. (I Corinthians 14:31)

This type of prophecy helps others grow and is available to any believer:

> But one who prophesies speaks to men for edification and exhortation and consolation. (I Corinthians 14:3)

The purpose of this type of prophecy is not foretelling or forth telling as in the ministry gift of prophecy, but for edification:

The Wind That Never Changes

> So also you, since you are zealous of spiritual gifts, seek to abound for the edification of the church. (I Corinthians 14:12)

Since the Corinthian church had given too much emphasis to the gift of tongues, Paul is trying to bring a balance in their public worship. If they want to excel in a spiritual gift, grow in prophecy. Learn how to listen to the Holy Spirit for words and acts of encouragement to others. A believer does not need the gift of teaching to teach others about Jesus. Nor does a believer need the gift of being an evangelist to lead someone to faith in Jesus. So also, a person does not have to have the gift of prophecy to be used of the Holy Spirit to speak edification, exhortation, and consolation to others.

To speak this way to others is the normal Christian life. Believers who do not even believe in modern day prophetic utterance do this all the time. They do it because they have the Holy Spirit, and He will use them to encourage others even when they do not know they are doing it. Think about the times someone says, "What you said to me the other day really blessed and encouraged me." In many cases, the believer who spoke the encouraging word does not even remember what they said. This is the Holy Spirit ministering the life of Jesus to others. Paul's exhortation in I Corinthians 14 is for believers to grow in this type of prophecy.

One final point on prophecy:

> And the spirits of prophets are subject to prophets; for God is not a God of confusion but of peace, as in all the churches of the saints. (I Corinthians 14:32–33)

Paul is giving specific instructions to believers not to allow emotion or human spirit to take over in the process of giving a prophecy. Many prophecies coming from humans will not be 100 percent pure to what the Holy Spirit is saying through that person. An element of the person's human spirit and emotions may color the prophecy. One of the reasons prophecy has such a bad reputation is some of the overly-emotional and human-spirit-contaminated behavior and attitudes some believers allow in their ministry to others.

> Therefore, my brethren, desire earnestly to prophesy, and do not forbid to speak in tongues. But all things must be done properly and in an orderly manner. (I Corinthians 14:39–40)

Properly means according to the Lord's commandments. *In an orderly manner* means not distorted by human emotion or opinions. These instructions from the Lord do not only apply to tongues and prophecy, but to all spiritual gifts.

Gift of Healing

The five most important gifts of the Holy Spirit in priority order are apostles, prophets, evangelists, pastors, and teachers (Ephesians 4:11). These five spiritual gifts are public ministry gifts given specifically "for the equipping of the saints for the work of service, to the building up of the body of Christ" (Ephesians 4:12). The gift of healing is not as important as the first five gifts of public ministry. Actually, there is no biblical method to rank the rest of the spiritual gifts in order of importance except the gift of tongues, which is last in importance (I Corinthians 12:28). This is strange, given that tongues gets so much press and attention on both sides of the argument. Similar to tongues, the spiritual gift of healing gets a disproportionate amount of attention. Some believers want to use supernatural healing as a demonstration and validation of God's love and power in the present day. The same argument is also used for seeking the gift of tongues to prove a person is filled with the Holy Spirit.

> This is the only thing I want to find out from you: did you receive the Spirit by the works of the Law, or by hearing with faith? (Galatians 3:2)

Seeking a sign or tangible physical evidence of God's approval or power violates the biblical commandment that believers are to walk by faith and not by sight (II Corinthians 5:7). God does give signs and wonders by the power of the Holy Spirit for His glory, purpose, and Kingdom. He commands His children to believe and trust His love and power without supernatural signs.

As Jesus said to Thomas,

> Because you have seen Me, have you believed? Blessed are they who did not see, and yet believed. (John 20:29)

Loving Jesus without seeing Him, or having supernatural confirmations in the midst of suffering, is the pinnacle of maturity as a Christian:

> In this you greatly rejoice, even though now for a little while, if necessary, you have been distressed by various trials, so that the proof of your faith, being more precious than gold which is perishable, even though tested by fire, may be found to result in praise and glory and honor at the revelation of Jesus Christ; and though you do not see Him now, but believe in Him, you greatly rejoice with joy inexpressible and full of glory, obtaining as the outcome of your faith the salvation of your souls. (I Peter 1:6–9)

This *salvation of your souls* is not being born again. Peter covers being born again in I Peter 1:3. This salvation is the culmination of faith by entering into His rest (Hebrews 4:10).

Healing gets so much attention, similar to apostles and prophets, because it is controversial. One reason it is controversial is that some use the gift of healing for personal gain:

> And constant friction between men of depraved mind and deprived of the truth, who suppose that godliness is a means of gain. (I Timothy 6:5)

Not much has changed in two thousand years. In Paul's day, some preached Christ of envy and strife and some used spiritual gifts for personal gain. It is the same in the present day. Not only so, but some actually fake supernatural healing to gain a following and increase monetary contributions to their ministry. To know that such things go on is not a valid argument against supernatural healing. There is a biblical gift of healing from the Holy Spirit and it does operate in the present day. However, like all spiritual gifts, it must operate under the Lordship of Christ for the glory of God alone. There is a temptation to exalt the sign gifts and draw attention to the gifts rather than the Giver. This is a major error. Remember that Jesus gave only two actions that would speak to the world: love and unity in His church. All the spiritual gifts are to accomplish this purpose.

Growing in Spiritual Gifts

Spiritual gifts are given according to the will of God:

> But to each one is given the manifestation of the Spirit for the common good. But now God has placed the members, each one of them, in the body, just as He desired. (I Corinthians 12:7, 18)

Many believers wonder about their spiritual gift. They believe each has a spiritual gift, but cannot determine their own spiritual gift. There is one main reason for this confusion: a believer has not had the correct teaching regarding growing up in Jesus. They think salvation is the end of the story. They are truly born again, have been baptized in the Holy Spirit and water, and stop right there. They are not taught that this is the beginning of their spiritual journey, not the end:

> Therefore, putting aside all malice and all deceit and hypocrisy and envy and slander, like newborn babies, long for the pure milk of the word, so that by it you may grow in respect to salvation, if you have tasted the kindness of the Lord. (I Peter 2:1–3)

> Do not lie to one another, since you laid aside the old self with its evil practices. (Colossians 3:9)

> But speaking the truth in love, we are to grow up in all aspects into Him who is the head, even Christ. (Ephesians 4:15)

There are three distinct levels in the Christian life. These three levels are given in I John 2:12–14 as "little children," "young men," and "fathers." Little children have their sins forgiven and know God as Father. Young men are strong in the word of God and have overcome the evil one. Fathers have known him who is from the beginning in an intimate and personal way. The three levels could also be understood as knowing Jesus is Savior, Lord, and Life. These three levels are illuminated by studying the tabernacle as described in the book of Exodus.

The tabernacle had three sections: courtyard, holy place, and holy of holies. Each section of the tabernacle had a source of light. In the courtyard, which had no covering, the light was sunlight. Think of this as the light of the natural man. In the holy place was the menorah. This was a candelabrum with seven lamps burning olive oil. It represents the word of God. The holy place had a thick covering and veil that blocked any sunlight. In the holy of holies, the light was God Himself appearing above the mercy seat between the two cherubim of gold as a luminous cloud of fire (Leviticus 16:2). Like the holy place, the holy of holies had a thick covering and a veil. Both the holy place and holy of holies would be completely dark if not for the candelabrum in the holy place and Presence of God as fire in the holy of holies.

The Couryard

When a person first comes to know Jesus as Savior, they figuratively enter into the courtyard of the tabernacle. They are born again by the Spirit of God. This is a large, open space, and the light is natural light. Allegorically, this represents a new Christian who has been living their life up to now by the flesh, the world and the devil. They bring in a lot of baggage into their new life from their old life. Initially, their perspective is mostly natural, not spiritual:

> But the natural man does not accept the things of the Spirit of God, for they are foolishness to him, and he cannot understand them, because they are spiritually appraised. (I Corinthians 2:14)

In the courtyard with other believers, the new Christian begins to learn what it means and how it works to walk in the Holy Spirit. They begin transitioning from a flesh-dominated Christian walk to a spiritual Christian walk:

> And I, brethren, could not speak to you as to spiritual men, but as to men of flesh, as to infants in Christ. (I Corinthians 3:1)

Using the Corinthian church as an example, there was doctrinal division, immorality, lawsuits with each other, pride, misusing spiritual gifts, etc. In other words, the Corinthians church was dominated by the flesh rather than Holy Spirit.

> If we live by the Spirit, let us also walk by the Spirit. (Galatians 5:25)

The Corinthians were alive by the Spirit, but as a church, they had not learned to walk by the Spirit. Sadly, most Christians spend their entire life in the courtyard. *Holiness in character is the exception rather than the rule.* They are never taught or challenged to go further in the Christian life or see examples of Christians who do. Being born again by the Spirit of God is wonderful and life changing. It is the beginning, like a baby that has just been born naturally. There is much more to the Christian life than having sins forgiven and a reservation in Heaven (I Peter 1:4). God intends that His children grow to know Him and develop Holy character in worshiping and serving Him (Philippians 3:10). In the courtyard, new believers in Jesus are introduced to the fundamentals of the Christian life:

> They were continually devoting themselves to the apostles' teaching and to fellowship, to the breaking of bread and to prayer. (Acts 2:42)

These four things are like the four legs of a stool. All are needed for balance and health in the Christian life. The Word of God, fellowship, Lord's supper, and prayer are fundamental.

There is another aspect of growing up as a believer in Jesus that does not get much attention: the necessity of suffering. Suffering is a normal experience for the Christian. Scripture mentions suffering many times but it is not a subject covered in many sermons or Bible studies. The primary cause of suffering as a Christian comes from the conflict between the desires of human nature and the Holy Spirit. The Father will often cause or allow events to happen in the life of His children that they do not expect or understand. Disappointments, reversals, lost opportunities, persecution, sickness, hardships, unmet needs/wants, and difficulties are just a few examples. Somehow, people get the idea that now that we really have an "in" with God that He is a type of spiritual Santa Claus who is there to meet our every need and want. Our Father does want to bless us and give us an abundant life as Jesus promised (John 10:10).

However, human nature does not know what abundant life looks like from God's perspective. When Peter tried to talk Jesus out of embracing the cross how did Jesus reply?

> Peter took Him aside and began to rebuke Him, saying, "God forbid it, Lord! This shall never happen to you." But He turned and said to Peter, "Get behind me, Satan! You are a stumbling block to me; for you are not setting your mind on God's interests, but man's." (Matthew 16:22–23)

Human nature will never learn or submit to God's interest if everything always goes well and meets expectations. Just like Jesus, His followers learn obedience through suffering:

> Although He was a Son, He learned obedience from the things which He suffered. (Hebrews 5:8)

> And He was saying to them all, If anyone wishes to come after Me, he must deny himself, and take up his cross daily and follow me. (Luke 9:23)

The cross is an instrument of death. Jesus commands those who are serious about being His disciples to follow His example and embrace the cross. How does this work? Suppose someone deliberately hurts a person. The hurt person has some Holy Spirit inspired choices. Forgiveness from the heart is the first step to take. Second, the emotions of outrage, anger, desire to hurt back, feelings of unfairness, etc., are surrendered to Jesus. The true disciple of Jesus recognizes that all the fleshly-inspired negative responses to hurtful treatment died on the cross with Jesus. By faith, the believer agrees with God.

> For you have died and your life is hidden with Christ in God. (Colossians 3:3)

Taking up one's cross is the acknowledgment that the negative emotions motivated by hurtful actions of others are not to be entertained and acted on, but denied as not part of us anymore. Jesus gave us the perfect example to follow:

> For you have been called for this purpose, since Christ also suffered for you, leaving you an example for you to follow in His steps, Who committed no sin, nor was any deceit found in His mouth; and while being reviled, He did not revile in return; while suffering, He uttered no threats, but kept entrusting Himself to Him who judges righteously; and He Him-

self bore our sins in His body on the cross, so that we might die to sin and live to righteousness; for by His wounds you were healed. (I Peter 3:21–24)

Following Jesus is to live redemptively:

> Those who hate me without a cause are more than the hairs of my head;
> Those who would destroy me are powerful, being wrongfully my enemies;
> What I did not steal, I then have to restore. (Psalm 69:4)

It is to recognize that the life of Jesus in us is there to love and forgive others and leave our rights to our Father. To do this requires death to self. This is what Paul means when he says, "Now I rejoice in my sufferings for your sake, and in my flesh I do my share on behalf of His body, which is the church, in filling up what is lacking in Christ's afflictions" (Colossians 1:24). The call of Christ is a call to die. As a believer is willing to die to himself, he will find the resurrection life of Christ being more and more expressed in his earthly life. There is no greater joy and fulfillment!

> All discipline for the moment seems not to be joyful, but sorrowful; yet to those who have been trained by it, afterwards it yields the peaceful fruit of righteousness. (Hebrews 12:11)

The courtyard is a training ground. A believer begins to learn to walk by the Holy Spirit more and more instead of walking according to the flesh. If the believer is trained by the discipline of the Heavenly Father, they begin to learn what real righteousness looks like:

> Do nothing from selfishness or empty conceit, but with humility of mind regard one another as more important than yourselves; do not merely look out for your own personal interest, but also for the interests of others. Have this attitude in yourselves, which was also in Christ Jesus, who, although He existed in the form of God, did not regard equality with God a thing to be grasped, but emptied Himself, taking the form of a bond-servant, and being made in the likeness of men. Being found in appearance as a man, He humbled Himself by becoming obedient to the point of death, even death on a cross. (Philippians 2:3–8)

The Holy Place

In the courtyard, a believer begins to learn what it means to know Jesus is Savior. Suffice it to say there is much more, and the holy place is the next step. Jesus is Lord:

> That I may know Him and the power of His resurrection and the fellowship of His sufferings, being conformed to His death; in order that I may attain to the resurrection from the dead. (Philippians 3:10–11)

In the holy place, a believer grows in knowing God intimately. It is no longer a matter of just saying yes to the Holy Spirit and no to the flesh. God's top priority is a relationship with His children. Service is important. The best service to God flows out of a relationship with God. In the holy place, His heart becomes the believer's heart. Like the courtyard, this process takes time. By seeking to know Him—His power, sufferings, and death—Paul's ultimate goal is living in the power of resurrection life. This is clear from the verses that follow Philippians 3:11. In the holy place, the believer grows in maturity as a child of God. This is a goal. Perfection is not possible in this life. As Paul says, "I press on toward the goal for the prize of the upward call of God in Christ Jesus" (Philippians 3:14).

In the holy place there are three items: the candelabrum, the altar of incense, and the showbread. Since the holy place has a thick covering and veil for the entrance, the only light source is the candelabrum. Only the high priest and his sons could enter the holy place. They also had to be ceremonially clean. For the believer, this means no unconfessed sin (I John 1:8-10). They went in to trim the lamps, burn incense, and maintain the showbread. Allegorically speaking, these activities represent the Holy Spirit teaching the believer the Word of God (I John 2:27), the Holy Spirit inspiring prayer and worship (Romans 8:26–27), and the Holy Spirit teaching the believer how to feed from the Living Bread, Jesus (John 6:48). The holy place is for learning intimacy in worship. It is a place of transformation:

> Therefore I urge you, brethren, by the mercies of God, to present your bodies a living and holy sacrifice, acceptable to God, which is your spiritual service of worship. And do not be conformed to this world, but be

transformed by the renewing of your mind, so that you may prove what the will of God is, that which is good and acceptable and perfect. (Romans 12:1–2)

All the animal sacrifices of temple worship not only speak of the sacrifice of Jesus on the cross, but also the identification of the believer in the sacrifice of Jesus as discussed in Essay II on baptism. This is why Paul calls this activity a living and holy sacrifice. Living sacrifice is an oxymoron: a sacrifice that lives but dies.

In the holy place the believer learns what it means to worship God in spirit and truth:

> God is spirit, and those who worship Him must worship in spirit and truth (John 4:24).

To worship this way requires and demands death to self (Luke 9:23). It is coming apart from the crowd, being alone with God, and learning to be in His presence. There can be no distractions. It requires coming apart and waiting on God alone. Holy place prayer and worship are not to be done while doing something else as driving a car or exercising or walking. These are fine and should be done by the believer. However, it is not worship in the holy place. Holy place worship is solitary, quiet, focused. It is a place to quiet the mind and heart and focus on God alone. At first there will be many distractions arising in the mind and heart. It takes time to learn how to be quiet before God and hear His voice.

Life in the holy place is walking in the Spirit under the direction and power of the Word of God:

> Your Word is a lamp to my feet and a light to my path. (Psalm 119:105)

> But we all, with unveiled face, beholding as in a mirror the glory of the Lord, are being transformed into the same image from glory to glory, just as from the Lord, the Spirit. (II Corinthians 3:18)

In the holy place, a believer is transformed more and more into the image of Christ by the word of God, prayer, and learning to spiritually feed on Jesus. The influence of the natural man decreases as the influence of the new spiritual man in Jesus increases. As discussed in Essay II, Israel in the wilderness for forty years is an allegory for an individual believer. After the national water baptism in the Red Sea (Exodus 14), the generation that grew up in Egypt does nothing but complain constantly and shows no real evidence of trusting or knowing God. For the next forty years, they are commanded by God to wander in the wilderness. They walked by the light of the pillar of cloud by day and pillar of fire by night. When the pillar stopped, they stopped. When the pillar moved, they moved. Where the pillar went, they went. This represents learning to walk in the light of the Word of God as taught by the Holy Spirit (John 16:13). God gave them manna to eat every day for forty years—supernatural food that represents eating Jesus, the Bread of Life:

> As the living Father sent Me, and I live because of the Father, so he who eats Me, he also will live because of Me. This is the bread which came down out of heaven; not as the fathers ate and died; he who eats this bread will live forever. (John 6:57–58)

Finally, the nation of Israel learned prayer and worship performing all the sacrifices that were part of Tabernacle service as taught in the book of Exodus. These three things in the national life of Israel in the wilderness for forty years—the cloud, the manna, and the Tabernacle service—correspond to the candelabrum, showbread, and incense altar of the holy place. Over those forty years, the generation that grew up in Egypt died, and a new generation that grew up under the tutelage of God came into being. For the believer in Jesus, this represents the death of the old man and the emergence of the new man in Jesus. This is the transformation that happens in the holy place. In the holy place, the believer learns and experiences intimacy with God that could not happen in the courtyard. *Holiness in character becomes the rule rather than the exception.*

Holy place training is not supposed to be easy on the flesh nature. It is difficult and orchestrated by God uniquely for each of His children. Consider the children of Israel in the wilderness:

> You shall remember all the way which the Lord your God has led you in the wilderness these forty years, that He might humble you, testing you, to know what was in your heart, whether you would keep His commandments or not. He humbled you and let you be hungry, and fed you with manna which you did not know, nor did your fathers know, that He might make you understand that man does not live by bread alone, but man lives by everything that proceeds out of the mouth of the Lord. He led you through the great and terrible wilderness, with its fiery serpents and scorpions and thirsty ground where there was no water; He brought water for you out of the rock of flint. In the wilderness He fed you manna which your fathers did not know, that He might humble you and that He might test you, to do good for you in the end. (Deuteronomy 8:2–3, 15–16)

> All discipline for the moment seems not to be joyful, but sorrowful; yet to those who have been trained by it, afterwards it yields the peaceful fruit of righteousness. (Hebrews 12:11)

God's goal in spiritual training is to teach His children by allowing trial and testing to come into their lives and then let them learn by experience that He is their Provider. He creates hunger and thirst that only He can satisfy with Himself. Learning in this arena of life produces suffering in the believer, as has been discussed. Growing up in Jesus will include suffering. It is unavoidable. Many times other believers will not understand the deep suffering of others. It has been called "The Dark Night of the Soul." It is understood only by experience. It cannot be described in such a way that someone could understand. It is deep and personal between the believer and his God.

> Why are you in despair, O my soul? And why have you become disturbed within me? Hope in God, for I shall again praise Him for the help of His presence. Deep calls to deep at the sound of Your waterfalls; all your breakers and your waves have rolled over me. (Psalm 42:5, 7)

Such trials and testing in life drive the believer to the word of God, worshipful prayer, and Jesus the Bread of Life. Victory is won when the believer is alone with God, seeking Him with all their heart (Jeremiah 29:11–13).

The Holy of Holies

The final step in the maturation of a believer in Jesus is the holy of holies: Jesus is Life. Only the high priest could enter the holy of holies. He could enter only once a year on the Day of Atonement. He had very specific commandments as to how he would enter (Leviticus 16). The light in the holy of holies is the Presence of God Himself as a flaming fire over the mercy seat. It is a supernatural light. The Ark of the Covenant held the Ten Commandments written on two stone tablets by the finger of God. Once a year the high priest would go inside the veil and sprinkle blood on the mercy seat covering the ark. The symbolism is that the blood of the sacrifice was positioned between the holy presence of God and God's righteous Ten Commandments. No one can keep the Ten Commandments. The first one is the most difficult:

You shall have no other gods before me. (Exodus 20:3)

The most influential god in a human heart is the will. If the will of a believer is more influential over life decisions that the living God, then personal will is an idol. This is the most common god in human experience. The only Person who did not have this idol in His heart is Jesus. All the rest of humanity wrestles with this idol constantly. The blood of the sacrifice is sprinkled on the mercy seat, which positions the blood between God and His commandments. This is salvation. The sacrifice of Jesus on the cross by shedding His perfect blood for the sins of mankind places His blood between God the Father and sinful humanity. Therefore, when God the Father looks at redeemed humanity, He sees through the blood of Jesus and does not see sin. This benefit is imputed to every person who repents, believes, and receives the merits of the sacrifice that Jesus made one the cross. People who persist in their willful rebellion and reject God's love in Jesus do not receive this benefit (John 3:36).

When Jesus died on the cross, one of the events that happened is that the veil in the temple that separated the holy place from the holy of holies ripped into two parts from top to bottom (Matthew 27:51). This signified that the sacrifice of Jesus on the cross and His death opened the way for believers in Jesus to enter into the holy of holies. This does not mean that a believer in Jesus is supposed to go to the temple and casually go into the holy of holies. For one thing, there is no temple standing in the present day. It means much more than just getting to go into the holy of holies and see the fire of the presence of God. God is saying that now that the sin issue is finished, eternal redemption has been accomplished by the sacrifice of Jesus on the cross (Hebrews 9:11-12). God's plan and desire is that His children be able to come into His glorious Presence and experience Him even in this life! He chooses when and where this happens according to His own will.

The best way to understand this is by examples. It is like Peter, James, and John on the Mount of Transfiguration with Jesus and entering into the cloud and hearing the Voice of God the Father. The Presence of God overwhelmed them (Luke 9:28-36). Paul was caught up to the third Heaven and heard words that a man is not permitted to speak (II Corinthians 12:2-4). Not every experience in the Presence of God by a believer is as profound as the examples given. Sometimes it is an overwhelming sense of Jesus Himself in the room with the believer. To experience this is a combination of reverence, wonder, awe, and delight, and sometimes overpowering emotion. These words do not do justice to what it is like to experience the Presence of God. Words cannot describe it. We cannot make this happen. God parts the torn veil at times He chooses to give His children a glimpse of Glory. He does it for His purposes, which we may not understand. It is not done casually.

In addition, it is not something that should be sought after just for the sake of a supernatural experience. Believers are commanded to walk by faith and not by sight. Seeking supernatural confirmations is not walking by faith. The point is that Jesus has made a way for us to be in the actual Presence of God because we are clean before Him. When He chooses to reveal Himself in a supernatural way to one of His children is completely up to Him. If God chooses to reveal Himself in this way to one of His children, the experience is life changing and never forgotten. It does not result in pride but rather humility and thanksgiving. It has the effect of making one forget himself in the majesty of God.

To conclude the discussion on spiritual growth for the believer in Jesus, it is helpful to consider two passages of scripture in the New Testament. First, Ephesians 3:14–19 is a prayer that Paul has for the Ephesian church as well as for all believers in Jesus. In this prayer, Paul mentions three levels of love: "rooted in love," "grounded in love," and "knowing the love of Christ which surpasses knowledge." These three levels of love correspond to the courtyard, holy place, and holy of holies of the Tabernacle in the Wilderness. Essay II discussed being rooted and grounded in love. Of particular note is the love corresponding to the holy of holies. Paul uses the word *know*, which is the most intimate form of knowing something and carries the connotation of being one with something. It is the same word used for the relationship between husband and wife. It is the deepest and highest level of knowing. Paul further states that this love "surpasses knowledge." It cannot be understood or explained with words. This is a clear reference to holy of holies life in Jesus. It is beyond description.

Second,

> Blessed be the God and Father of our Lord Jesus Christ, who according to His great mercy has caused us to be born again to a living hope through the resurrection of Jesus Christ from the dead, to an inheritance which is imperishable and undefiled and will not fade away, reserved in heaven for you, who are protected by the power of God through faith for a salvation ready to be revealed in the last time. In this you greatly rejoice, even though now for a little while, if necessary, you have been distressed by various trials, so that the proof of your faith, being more precious than gold which is perishable, even though tested by fire, may be found to result in praise and glory and honor and the revelation of Jesus Christ; and though you have not seen Him now, but believe in Him, you greatly rejoice

> with joy inexpressible and full of glory, obtaining the outcome of your faith the salvation of your souls. (I Peter 1: 3–9)

The courtyard is in verses 3–5. Notice the words the Holy Spirit uses: *born again, living hope, inheritance, reserved in heaven, protected by the power of God, greatly rejoice*. These are initial salvation promises. The holy place is in verses 6 and 7: *distressed, trials, proof of your faith, tested by fire, praise and glory and honor*. These are holy place or wilderness experiences. The holy of holies is in verses 8 and 9: *greatly rejoice, joy inexpressible, full of glory, outcome of your faith*. The last phrase, *outcome of your faith*, means the goal or ultimate result, similar to what Paul says in Philippians 3:10. The word *inexpressible* is similar to *surpasses knowledge* in the Ephesians passage above. It is the same meaning as the word Paul uses in II Corinthians 12:4 describing his time in the third heaven.

The purpose of this rather long and detailed discussion of what it means "to grow up in all aspects into Him who is the head, even Christ" (Ephesians 4:15) is to illuminate the process that God uses to perfect His children. There is so much more than going to church, reading the Bible, praying, and trying to be a good person.

> This is eternal life, that they may know You, the only true God, and Jesus Christ whom you have sent. (John 17:3)

The word *know* in this verse is the same word discussed above. To be intimately one with God. This is the goal of the believer in Jesus: to know Him! Out of knowing Him everything else flows. This is the reason some believers do not know their spiritual gift. Their knowledge of Jesus is not mature. Paul describes this:

> And I, brethren, could not speak to you as to spiritual men, but as to men of flesh, infants in Christ. I gave you milk to drink, not solid food; for you were not yet able to receive it. Indeed, even now you are not yet able, for you are still fleshly. For since there is jealousy and strife among you, are you not fleshly, and are you not walking like mere men? (I Corinthians 3:1–3)

One last example that vividly shows the contrast between immature character and mature character in Jesus:

> Who among you is wise and understanding? Let him show by his good behavior his deeds in the gentleness of wisdom. But if you have bitter jealousy and selfish ambition in your heart, do not be arrogant and so lie against the truth. This wisdom is not that which comes down from above, but is earthly, natural, demonic. For where jealousy and selfish ambition exist, there is disorder and every evil thing. But the wisdom from above is first pure, then peaceable, gentle, reasonable, full of mercy and good fruits, unwavering, without hypocrisy. And the seed whose fruit is righteousness is sown in peach by those who make peace. (James 3:13–18)

The believer who walks in the "wisdom from above" knows the Father through the Son in the power of the Holy Spirit.

This discussion on spiritual gifts did not cover all the spiritual gifts. The intent was to point out that all believers have at least one spiritual gift, and the primary way to discover one's gift is to "seek His kingdom and His righteousness" (Mathew 6:33). It is very important to realize that proper working of all the spiritual gifts depends on the believer's submission to the Lordship of Christ in using the gift. This is the most important factor in ministering any spiritual gift, and especially the sign gifts. With regard to the sign gifts and whether they ceased around 100 AD, each believer needs to be like the Jews of Berea (Acts 17:11) and search the scriptures in the Holy Spirit to decide for themselves what they believe. Whichever way they decide, all believers should "speak the truth in love" (Ephesians 4:15) and be gracious and tolerant with other believers with whom they disagree. In learning to be a disciple of Jesus, there is nothing more important than walking in love (I Corinthians 13:1–3).

The final topic with regard to spiritual gifts is the fact that God does not always fulfill our expectations, even though they seem to be biblical to our understanding. As an example, many believers have asked the question why some are not healed when prayed for in faith. The simple answer is that there is no answer in this life. Scripture clearly teaches that some have the gift of healing (I Corinthians 12:9), and believers in general are encouraged to pray for the sick (James 5:13–16). Many are healed but some are not. It is easy to blame a lack of faith when this happens. However, there have been many cases where faith was not lacking and yet healing did not happen.

Smith Wigglesworth's daughter Alice remained deaf all her life, even though many deaf people received healing under Wigglesworth's ministry (5). Charles H. Spurgeon, "Prince of Preachers," was a great man of faith yet struggled with depression his entire life (6). Mrs. Charles E. Cowman, who wrote *Streams in the Desert*, ministered to her husband for six years as he slowly died of heart failure (7). She and her husband strongly believed in divine healing and sought it diligently. It was not to be. During those trying six years, Mrs. Cowman wrote *Streams*, which is one of the most beloved and widely read devotionals the world has ever seen. While sick, her husband, Charles, spent long years praying over maps of the world for the Lord to send missionaries with the gospel. Mrs. Cowman recounts that all his prayers were answered after his death.

Is it possible to conclude that if the Lord had healed Charles early on in his illness, that the world would never have had the gift of *Streams in the Desert*? Or, no countries that for years Charles fervently prayed for would have had the gospel? More unanswerable questions.

A little insight from Hebrews 11:33–38. Some experienced supernatural intervention such as delivery from death, stopping the mouths of lions, quenching the power of fire, and resurrection from the dead. All in faith. Others experienced torture, mockings, imprisonment, death, destitution, homelessness. Again, all in faith. It would seem that faith would consistently produce supernatural intervention and stop trials and tribulation, including physical death. God is in control, and it is His supernatural intervention in all circumstances in the lives of His children, whether it goes according to their expectations or not. There are many interpretations about Paul's thorn in the flesh (II Corinthians 12:7), Timothy's chronic stomach problems (I Timothy 5:23), or why the Apostle Paul left Trophimus at Melitus sick (II Timothy 4:20). Many interpretations but no definitive conclusions, at least not to the point where there is universal agreement.

> Who is there who speaks and it comes to pass, unless the Lord has commanded it? Is not from the mouth of the Most High that both good and ill go forth? (Lamentation 3:37-38)

> For from Him and through Him and to Him are all things. To Him be the glory forever. Amen. (Romans 11:36)

Whatever God decides to do in any situation is good. It has to be because God is good and only God is good. Whether it is good from the natural or human perspective is not relevant when it comes to trusting God. In this life, God is not pleased to allow His children to know as they are known (I Corinthians 13:12). This is a large part of what it requires to "walk by faith, not by sight" (II Corinthians 5:7), much less to walk by the limits of our own understanding.

> Trust in the Lord with all your heart and do not lean on your own understanding, (Proverbs 3:5)

The difference in knowledge and understanding between the smallest virus and a human being is not even close to the much greater difference between a human being and infinite God—an infinite Holy God that defines and personifies perfect love, knowledge, wisdom, power, glory, goodness, and truth! The same infinitely perfect God commands His children to trust in His character that whatever He does, it is good, acceptable, and perfect (Romans 12:2). He does not owe any being in the spiritual or physical realms any explanations (Job 33:13). Jesus commands that believers in Him use their spiritual gifts for His glory and the benefit of His body, the Church. The effect of the gift is a decision of the Father. The believer's goal is to do the will of the Father:

> Not everyone who says to Me, "Lord, Lord," will enter the kingdom of heaven, but he who does the will of my Father who is in heaven will enter. (Matthew 7:21)

When it comes to spiritual gifts, which gifts, and how and when they work, His will is all that matters.

The Unpardonable Sin

> Truly I say to you, all sins shall be forgiven the sons of men, and whatever blasphemies they utter; but whoever blasphemes against the Holy Spirit never has forgiveness, but is guilty of an eternal sin – because they were saying, "He has an unclean spirit." (Mark 3:28–30)

The religious leaders from Jerusalem had already made up their minds that Jesus of Nazareth could not possibly be the Messiah:

> They answered him, "You are not also from Galilee, are you? Search, and see that no prophet arises out of Galilee." (John 7:52)

> Therefore some of the Pharisees were saying, "This man is not from God, because He does not keep the Sabbath." (John 9:16)

For these and other uninformed reasons, the Jewish religious leaders rejected Jesus as the Messiah. However, they could not deny His supernatural power.

> Therefore the chief priests and the Pharisees convened a council, and were saying, "What are we doing? For this man is performing many signs." (John 11:47)

The only way they could explain His supernatural power was to attribute it to Satan:

> The scribes who came down from Jerusalem were saying, "He is possessed by Beelzebul," and "He casts out the demons by the ruler of the demons." (Mark 3:22)

Jesus replied,

> If I by Beelzebul cast out demons, by whom do your sons cast them out? For this reason they will be your judges. But if I cast out demons by the Spirit of God, then the kingdom of God has come upon you. (Matthew 12:27–28)

Every supernatural work that Jesus did was by the power of the Holy Spirit:

The Wind That Never Changes

> And Jesus returned to Galilee in the power of the Spirit, and news about Him spread through all the surrounding district. (Luke 4:14)

> If I alone testify about Myself, My testimony is not true. There is another who testifies of Me, and I know that the testimony which He gives about Me is true. (John 5:31-32)

In this verse, Jesus is referring to the testimony given by the Holy Spirit that He is the Christ. The supernatural works that Jesus performed in the power of the Holy Spirit were a validation by the Father that He was the Christ. To reject the testimony of the Father by the Holy Spirit was to reject the Father, Jesus, and the Holy Spirit. The Jewish religious leaders not only rejected the testimony of the Holy Spirit but also attributed the works of the Holy Spirit to the ruler of the demons. The unpardonable sin is to reject the testimony about Jesus from the Holy Spirit.

The Holy Spirit is God's final and greatest revelation of Himself to Israel and humanity in general. God the Father revealed Himself to Israel as fire and a Voice on Mount Sinai (Exodus 19). Ultimately, Israel rejected God the Father. God the Son revealed Himself to Israel by His life and on the cross (John 19). As a nation, Israel rejected God the Son. God the Holy Spirit revealed Himself to Israel on the day of Pentecost (Acts 2). From the day of Pentecost until the stoning of Stephen in Acts 7, the Holy Spirit was poured out in a much more powerful way than ever happened in the Old Testament because Jesus was glorified (John 7:39). Israel rejected the testimony of the Holy Spirit, and Stephen's complete summary of Israel's history in Acts 7 is a turning point. He finishes his summary with these words: "You men who are stiff necked and uncircumcised in heart and ears are always resisting the Holy Spirit; you are doing just as your fathers did" (Acts 7:51). This signifies that the gospel message, which was to be presented to the Jew first (Romans 1:16), was now going to focus on the gentiles. It is not coincidental that the first mention of Saul, the future apostle to the gentiles, occurs in Acts 7:58. From this point forward in the book of Acts, the focus of the gospel is on the gentiles. Many Jews did receive the gospel message and became followers of Jesus. However, as a nation, Israel rejects Jesus as Messiah to the present day. This summary of God's revelations of Himself to the nation of Israel gives the sense of what it means to blaspheme the Holy Spirit. *The Holy Spirit is God's final and greatest revelation of Himself to humanity.* Rejection of the Holy Spirit's testimony about Jesus leaves a person with no hope of salvation.

A person who has committed the unpardonable sin has no concern about salvation and does not worry about it. The following passage describes this heart attitude:

> But the Spirit explicitly says that in later times some will fall away from the faith, paying attention to deceitful spirits and doctrines of demons, by means of the hypocrisy of liars seared in their conscience as with a branding iron. (I Timothy 4:1–2)

A conscience seared as with a branding iron. A person with a willful hardened heart will not come to repentance (Hebrews 6:6). If a person worries or is concerned about having committed the unpardonable sin, this is a sure indication that the heart is not hardened beyond repentance. Satan often tries to convince a believer that they have committed the unpardonable sin. This is surprisingly common. Concern about having committed the unpardonable sin is a sure indication that the believer has not committed this sin. Those who have committed the unpardonable sin do not care.

NOTES

1. Brother Yun, *The Heavenly Man*, (Kregel Publications, 2002).

2. Corrie ten Boom, *The Hiding Place*, (Chosen Books, 2006).

3. Darlene Deibler Rose, *Evidence Not Seen: A Woman's Miraculous Faith in the Jungles of World War II*, (Harper Collins, 1990).

4. Corrie ten Boom, *Tramp For The Lord*, (JoveBooks, 1978).

5. Dr. Michael H. Yeager, *The Miracles of Smith Wigglesworth*, (CreateSpace Independent Publishing Platform, 2015)

6. Zack Eswine, *Spurgeon's Sorrows: Realistic Hope for Those Who Suffer from Depression*, (Christian Focus Publications, 2014).

7. B. H. Pearson, *The Vision Lives*, (OMS International, 1981).

ESSAY IV

Charles H Perry

Thou art All Fair my Love

Learning how Christ loves His Bride

Introduction

"The Song of Solomon" in the Bible is a love story between a husband and wife. It is also an allegory showing the love of Christ for His Church—a passionate narrative that describes how the lovers see and enjoy each other. Initially, the wife focuses on what she considers flaws in her character and physical being—various things she thinks make her less desirable (Song 1:5–6). The husband focuses on her beauty and how she captivates him. Eight times in the narrative he says, "Thou art all fair, my love." Twelve times he tells her she is beautiful. The husband's unconditional love, delight, and acceptance of his wife set her free from worrying about what she thinks are her defects. Over time, she realizes that he really does not regard as important the defects that she thinks she has. She discovers that his love satisfies her more than her desire to be without flaw. Her insecurities about herself are lost in her husband's delightful love for her. At the end of the story she says, "Then was I in his eyes as one that found peace" (Song 8:10). This is the key point of "Essay IV, Thou Art All Fair My Love." It tells the story of the husband-wife relationship and the relationship between Christ and His church: redemptive, unconditional love that sets one free (John 8:36).

Beginnings

My wife and I married on January 23, 1970. She was nineteen and I was eleven days from being twenty-six Now that I have raised two daughters and two sons, I totally agree that I robbed the cradle. However, we both believed our marriage was of God, and time has proven that out. My wife's family was well known in the small town where I went to college for my bachelor's degree. Her father was the Executive Vice President of the largest bank in town when we dated, and later became Chief Executive Office and head of that bank the same year we were married. Her maternal grandfather had served in the U. S. Congress. Members of her family had been in the local country club for two generations. It seemed to me at the time that everyone in her family was wealthy and important. We would visit her relatives, and I was impressed with their beautiful homes located in the best neighborhoods. I felt totally out of place in such settings but did a good job of hiding how I felt.

One little trick I used to bolster my wobbly self-confidence was to say to myself, "You have a lot of money, but I go to graduate school and am studying for a Ph.D." In other words, "You're rich, but I'm smart." This is a terrible thing to admit, but it was normal for me in those years. When I felt insecure, which was most of the time, I would look for some flaw in another person that would allow me to feel superior. It is a good thing that my future wife and her family did not know how messed up I was on the inside. I had no idea how messed up I was. But I am getting ahead of myself.

No one in my family had ever been a member of a country club. In fact, my father's family was a bit rough. One of my uncles was a barroom brawler who liked to pick fights. He had the reputation of being the roughest fighter in the town where I grew up. He was a short, stocky man, but he was muscular and fast. When he wasn't fighting he spent his time hunting, fishing, and occasionally, when he was drunk, terrorizing his family and others. I remember a day when my drunken uncle chased my daddy home, threating to hurt him. Dad raced through the front door and locked it behind him just as my uncle got to the front porch. My uncle began beating on the front door, cursing and screaming. My mother went to the front door and stood between my uncle and my father. For some reason, my uncle always respected my mother. She calmed him down, and he left. I was young when this happened, but I remember it vividly.

The Wind That Never Changes

Everyone was afraid of my uncle—everyone except another uncle who had been a professional boxer. The brawler uncle never messed with him. Another member of my father's family had been a hobo in his early life, and one of my aunts had the kind of life that the men tended to stand in small groups and whisper about.

My mother's family was completely different: poor but educated and refined. Her father was a country pastor, and his family reflected his vocation. All my aunts and uncles on my mother's side went to college. No one on my father's side had attended college. My mother's relatives lived a few miles outside of town, so their influence was minimal. We would visit them, but often without my father. My father would put on his best behavior when he would visit my mother's family. Actually, my father would put on his best behavior everywhere except at home with mom and me. He was very charming to others, but that charming side is something my mother and I rarely saw when he was home. Some in my father's family lived in our neighborhood, so I was influenced by them.

I was so disdainful of where I lived that I told people I lived in another neighborhood because I thought it sounded better. We lived in a poor, working class, mixed-race neighborhood. Since my mother and father both worked, I had a lot of unsupervised street time. By the age of nine I had logged a lot of discretionary time on the streets. I was exposed to things that no child should learn so early.

Sex was an ever present theme. Older kids in the neighborhood were into sex games and experimentations that I invariably saw and sometimes participated in. I also learned about rape, and how one of the teenage boys in the neighborhood wished he could have sex with my mother. The neighborhood was about as raw and ugly as possible, given that there was only alcohol in those days. Police raided a house very near to ours one night; we later learned it was a sex party. Two of the teenaged boys in the neighborhood sexually molested me. One of them introduced me to pornography. Mom and Dad never knew about the abuse.

I witnessed many fights. I stood by one day watching two women curse and threaten each other while holding butcher knives. A neighborhood boy died as result of a fight. The boy had significant health issues, but it was a shock. I watched one man knock down another man who was cursing him.

I was no angel. One day I tricked someone into eating dog poop. On another occasion I told some innocent kids to go in and curse out the maid staying with them for not giving them candy. These children were not like the rest of us in the neighborhood. I cringe today when I think of the horrible things I told those children to say. Not surprisingly, their parents kept them away from me. I learned to curse before the first grade, but never around my parents. Cursing in that neighborhood was so normal, nobody thought anything about it. Curse words were some of the first words kids in my neighborhood would say.

Because I was so shy and quiet, my first grade teacher decided that I was not too bright. She put me in what I called the "dumb group." I was smart enough to realize that the class was divided into two groups. The smart group got to do all the fun things, and the dumb group was just there. This stigma stuck with me all through grade school. After years of being considered dull, I decided that I was dumb, so I never tried. I retreated into a dream world. All my teachers would tell my parents, "If I could just get your son to stop daydreaming and listen." I guess my real world was so sad that I created another world to live in. In high school I read the short story, "The Secret Life of Walter Mitty." In this story Walter Mitty is a timid, quiet man who never stands up to anyone, especially his wife. He compensates his real-world emptiness by creating a dream world where he is an amazing person who is admired by everyone because he can do anything. I could really relate to Walter Mitty. My father's solution to my academic problems was to beat me with a wide, heavy belt. Yes, beat is the correct word. I would have red marks from my neck to my ankles. It seemed he was always in a bad mood and angry, especially about my

The Wind That Never Changes

school work.

In grammar school I had the same teacher in fifth grade that my father had. It didn't take long for her to decide that my academic performance was similar to my father's: bad. To make sure he knew how bad I was doing, she sent one of my failure papers home for him to sign. When I gave it to him he said, "I'll please sign your ass—get in the bathroom." I still remember that one. My whole childhood is a mosaic of my father's anger. Yelling, cursing, tearing up furniture, turning over a table full of food and sometimes hitting my mother were all just part of my early life. He threw a half brick at me one day as hard as he could. If I had not side stepped, it would have hit me square in the chest. Sometime I just had to run away till he cooled off. My mother would compensate for my father's physical and emotional abuse by over-protecting me. When it came to my school work, she would cry and beg. Nothing worked; I made bad grades until my senior year in high school and then only slightly better. By the way, my future wife was an honor student in high school and voted "Most likely to succeed." Just thought I would let you know.

When I was fifteen my family moved to another location, and I left all the sadness and pain of where I grew up behind, or so I thought. Hopefully, a new town, neighborhood, and school would make things better. My family's financial position was improved as my Dad got a new job, and money was less an issue. This did not change the sadness of my life. I did no better in school, academically or socially. It didn't take long for everyone, teachers and students, to write me off as a loser.

One day I let other boys talk me into locking an entire class in their room. It was a safety issue. Of course I got caught. The principal said, "You are not worth punishing!" Dad still had his violent temper at home, and Mom and Dad still had horrible, scary fights regularly. My childhood is characterized by going into the bedroom and praying that God would make my mom and dad stop fighting. They always did. I guess that was the beginning of my walk with God, even though I did not know Him.

I always believed in God, and my family was very religious. We attended church every Sunday. My father was a Sunday school teacher and part time preacher. He loved to quote and argue about the Bible. Since my mother's father was a minister, she was also very active in church. Neither my parents nor I had a personal relationship with the Lord Jesus in those early years. That happened later.

Several events happened in my junior year that began to wake me up. For some strange reason I decided to try out for the senior play. It was in the spring of our junior year, but it was still called the senior play. The person casting and directing the play was from a local college and didn't know I was a loser. I have always been a good reader and able to project myself confidently when speaking publicly. It is an odd situation that my teachers decided I was dull, but yet I was a different person in front of an audience—not shy, but outgoing and confident. My English teacher said she almost could not believe I was the same person when she saw me in the play.

I got the lead role, playing opposite one of the most popular girls in our class. All the cool, popular kids were in the play. I discovered that I could learn my lines as well or better than anyone. The girl I played opposite learned to depend on me as I learned her lines and mine. Maybe I was not dumb, so I began to try a little.

The only "A" I made in high school was in wood shop. My high school grade point average was 1.7—a "D". At the time, in 1962, the state college near where we lived had to take you if you graduated from high school. I just barely made it, as my father so disdainfully reminded me the morning after graduation. This was typical of our relationship: tense. He had no respect for me, and I felt likewise. I always had a love for my father, but I did not like him.

My mother and I were totally different. She and I had very similar temperaments and had grown very close emotionally. My father traveled a lot and was out of town during the week. Mom and I had lots of fun doing simple things like getting a coke and peanuts or hot doughnuts. When Dad was gone, our house was happy. He complained once that he felt like a stranger in his own home. In a sense that was true. When he was in a bad mood, which was most of the time, neither my Mom nor I could get along with him, so we just emotionally ignored him. However, in those rare moments when he was sweet, it was so easy to love him and enjoy being with him. I guess that is why I had some love for him. In hindsight I know what was wrong. My father was insecure about himself, supporting his family, and life in general. Anger is how he dealt with his insecurities. It makes me sad to remember those dark days. My mother told me later that she wanted to leave my father many times, but pride was the reason she didn't. Her father had told her before they married that her fiancé was the most overbearing man he had ever met. She had to live with her decision, and now I am glad she did.

I tried to get into several private colleges with no success. In the end, I decided to go to the state college that had the reputation at the time of "where you go when you can't get accepted anywhere else." I received the catalog, and the information included told me that I had to declare a major. One afternoon I remember thumbing through the college catalog, and my eyes fell on pre-med. "That's it," I said. "I will become a medical doctor." That is exactly how it happened. Don't ask me why. No thought of my poor grades, poor preparation, being dumb, no money.

My dad went to the bank and borrowed enough money to pay for one semester. I was a little surprised when he borrowed money to send me to college. I believe he always loved mom and me. However, his insecurities so dominated his emotions that his anger was what we saw most of the time. He said, "This is all I am giving you. You can go down there and earn a degree or come back home, and I will get you a job in construction. It's up to you."

I remember very well the night Mom and Dad dropped me off at my off-campus room. Mom cried, and I don't remember

Dad saying anything. Here I was, at last on my own. This was the turning point of my life. When I got away from Dad's abuse and Mom's over-protection, something clicked and suddenly woke up in me that I did not know was there. During freshman orientation, 1000 of us sat in a large room while the Dean of Students told us, "By Christmas half of you will be gone." I looked around at my classmates and said to myself, "Well, it ain't gonna be me." My first semester in pre-med I earned a 3.3 grade point average. This included a D in English. I made A's in chemistry, biology, and algebra, and two B's. Ironically, I had made F's in high school chemistry and algebra. I won a tuition scholarship that first semester that paid my tuition for four years.

My first off-campus room was three doors down from where my future wife was growing up. I walked by her house every day going to and from classes. At that time, she was twelve and I was eighteen Her brother used to come over to play with a child where I lived. I even remember seeing children playing in the yard behind the big iron fence around her house when I would walk by. Of course, I never thought for a second that my life and the life of the family living in this beautiful home would be intertwined.

Transformation

While my first year in college went well, the emotional wounds from my childhood were not gone. They began to be a problem my sophomore year when my grade point average for a semester dropped to a 2.2. The problems were anxiety and panic attacks. From my earliest memories I have always been a worrier. My Dad would travel and be out of town during the week. Mom worked and would get home around 5:30 every day. By the age of eight I would come in from school and have no one there to take care of me. In the winter when it got dark by 5:00, I would be afraid that something would happen to Mom, and she would not be home. All my life the most terrifying words in my imagination are, "But what if." Even by the age of eight I knew about rape from my street "education." Strange as it seems I would say to myself, "But what if someone kidnaps, rapes, and kills my mother?" That is a terrible emotional burden for an eight-year-old, but it was normal life for me. It was my constant fear, and I never told Mom. Every day it hung over me like a heavy dark cloud: "Would today be the day when she does not come home?" At that time my mother was my life. I remember one night in particular when she was not home by 6:00. I was in a rocking chair where I could see the driveway outside the window. I was beside myself, crying hysterically and beating the fabric of the chair with my fists in panic. I don't remember what I told her when she found me crying. She had stopped by the grocery store on the way home.

By the time I got to college my fears had switched over to my health. I was a hypochondriac. Cancer was my usual fear, but I worried about other ailments, usually terminal ones like lockjaw and rabies. Every ache or strange feeling would put me into an emotional tailspin. Any real or imagined lumps under my arms or on my neck were surely tumors. It almost seems funny now, looking back on how I worried irrationally about my health. I went to the clinic on campus so many times that the doctor once kicked me out. I suppose he was trying to shock me. It didn't work. I continued to worry and just didn't go back. I would be so panicky that I could not eat for days. Usually these spells would last about three days in which I could not eat or sleep. While waiting in a barber shop, I read an article on prostate cancer. Immediately I developed the symptoms, including a low fever. I am amazed how powerful fear-driven imagination can be. This episode again lasted about three days in which I could not eat or sleep. It never occurred to me that prostate cancer is almost non-existent in a twenty-year-old! This was typical, always completely irrational. After it was over, I was exhausted as if I had been recovering from an extended illness or had just run a marathon. It is surprising how draining panic can be. I remember one night holding on to the sides of the bed resisting the urge to run down the middle of the street screaming at 3:00 am. I discovered a really hot tub bath had a relaxing effect and calmed me down. I took a lot of really hot tub baths my sophomore year.

The anxiety was a little less my junior year, and my grades improved. I went to the school psychologist because I was concerned that I was not smart enough to be a medical doctor. He gave me an IQ test, and it turned out I was smart enough to be a medical doctor. I also told him of my anxiety and panic attacks. He gave me some tests and unofficially diagnosed me as having "free floating anxiety." He explained that I have these irrational fearful feelings or feelings of impending disaster, and then focus my fear on some object. It seemed to be true. I regularly felt anxious for no apparent reason. If there was no reason to feel anxious, I would invent one. In my early childhood it was my mother's safety; in college it was my health.

In the spring of my junior year I applied to medical school and was accepted. About the same time, I had started a part-time job in a research laboratory at a local Veterans Administration psychiatric hospital. My job was to build research apparatus such as a water maze for rats and various other mechanical and electrical devices. All my life I had been a tinkerer. By the time I was twelve I could fix just about anything around the house, and my mother would come to me instead of my father, who was not particularly good at repairs. I built my own stereo equipment and was generally quite comfortable with electrical and mechanical systems. I discovered in my research job that I loved the challenge of inventing something new or a new way to do something that had not been done before. I would work for hours even without pay just for the thrill of making something useful or novel out of surplus equipment. My boss, a Ph.D. clinical and research psychologist, was delighted with my ability, and my first published paper was a novel and improved way to quantitatively measure the physical activity of a small animal in a cage. It significantly improved the state of the art for such measurements. I enjoyed research so much that

The Wind That Never Changes

I decided that I would go to graduate school instead of medical school. It did not occur to me at the time that I could do medical research as a doctor. I declined my acceptance to medical school and changed my major to chemistry, since I had all the required courses for a degree.

By this time my relationship with my father had evolved into a mutual tolerance of each other. He was proud of my college accomplishments, but we still did not get along, and the relationship was still tense. His temper was as bad as ever. Because of this I was not impressed with what he told me just before Christmas in 1965. He came in one night when I was home for break and announced that he had been "born again." My reaction was disdain. I knew his brand of religion: teach the Bible on Sunday and terrorize your family the rest of the week. I looked at him and said, "That's good Dad," and turned from him and had a smirk on my face. I didn't dare give him a smirk look. I was too afraid of him. He went to bed, and I forgot what he told me.

In early 1966 I was home again for a weekend and my Mom came to me and said, "I am concerned about your father." She said he never lost his temper, was kind and gentle, and he stopped smoking. The first two observations were amazing enough—but stopped smoking! My father had smoked two to three packs a day for my entire life. His attitude was, "Hell, you got to die of something." The first time he let me drive alone was to get him a pack of cigarettes. He smoked the strong kind without a filter. Stopped smoking? I couldn't believe it! I started watching my father. I even tried to make him lose his temper by pushing some of his hot buttons. Nothing worked; he never got angry. It was like he was a different person. One day I discovered him crying and listening to Handel's Messiah on the stereo. My father never cried. He taught me not to cry. When I got spanked he never let me cry and would spank me till I stopped. I thought he had a heart condition, and the doctor told him if he did not stop smoking and losing his temper he would have a heart attack.

After a few more weekends of watching my father I finally went to him and said, "Dad, what has happened to you." He would not tell me. He wanted me to go with him to a meeting of businessmen on Saturday morning. It turned out to be a prayer meeting for men from different churches and denominations who came together every Saturday morning for breakfast, Bible-study, and prayer. The meetings were held at a rescue mission. It was an old house that had been modified to have a large meeting room, commercial kitchen and rooms for the homeless. The first time I walked in, it looked drab, and I wondered why the meetings were held in such a place.

The environment of the meeting room quickly lost significance when I noticed how the men were radiant in their faith. It really amazed me how they talked about Jesus—like they really knew and loved Him, not like an abstract, distant God of long ago or far away. This really fascinated me, so I started coming home every weekend to go to this meeting. Another discovery was that Dad was like them. He talked about Jesus like they did. I had not noticed him talking about Jesus at home, but his new behavior had gotten my attention.

After seeing the dramatic change in my father's life, and meeting with the other men every Saturday morning, a conflict began in my heart. I had always considered myself a Christian. My religious views were shaped by my maternal grandfather. He was a humble, unassuming country minister who had a reputation of preferring small churches. I remember him being very gentle and quiet spoken. He also impressed me as being very scholarly. Being around him and my grandmother was a respite from the turmoil of my own home. My grandfather never discussed Jesus with me. His life is what I remember, and I wanted to be like him. What really impressed me were the stories of how he forgave and loved people who hurt him and took advantage of his kind and giving ways. Other members of the family would tell these stories. He never did. He passed away when I was about twelve but my memories of him are vivid. Even at that age I remember saying to myself, "If anyone goes to

The Wind That Never Changes

heaven, it will be my grandfather."

From an early age I read the Bible every day, prayed every night, was active in Church, and believed that Jesus was the Son of God. At one point in my senior year in high school I even considered going to college to train for the ministry like my grandfather. The conflict about my being a Christian began about a month after I started attending the meetings on Saturday mornings, and continued to intensify. I kept saying to myself, "I am a Christian." When I was with the men on Saturday mornings, I listened to everything they had to say and studied their behavior. It never occurred to me that I was an observer and not a participant when they talked about the Jesus they knew, loved, and served.

Each Saturday morning someone would volunteer to bring the devotional for the next meeting. One particular morning nobody volunteered. By this time, I had idolized these men, and I found myself disappointed that no one agreed to take the next meeting. In my frustration, suddenly I volunteered to have the devotional for the next meeting. Later I asked myself, "What came over me? I don't know how to have a devotional for these men."

The following Friday evening I was home for the weekend. Since school was only thirty miles away and I had a girlfriend in the town where my parents lived, I came home most weekends. I had not yet prepared anything for the next morning. My father wanted me to go to a different meeting with him. For some reason I had a lot of anxiety about going. I made every excuse possible, including that I needed the time to get ready for tomorrow. Nothing worked. He insisted and said that I did not even have to get out of the car. I finally agreed to go, and we parked in front of the meeting place, which turned out to be the rescue mission. I had never been there for an evening meeting when the homeless attended. As I was sitting in the car waiting on my father to come back out, he stuck his head out the door and motioned for me to come in. I shook my head. He then gave me one of those looks that meant instant obedience that I had seen all my life. It didn't matter if I was eight or twenty-two as I was now. I was still afraid of my father. I got out of the car.

Inside he started excitedly introducing me to all these people I really did not want to meet. They were homeless street people who were attending the evening religious service so they could get a place to sleep and hot meals. This was a Christian rescue mission. Attending the service was a requirement for the bed and hot meals. The street people called it, "Three hots and a flop." Some of the street people had made a profession of faith in Christ and were working at the mission. These were the ones I had to meet. I did not like any of them. All I wanted to do was get out of there. Even though they were cleaned up, they still looked like street people. I did not like them and did not want to be there.

Dad wanted to stay for the meeting, and I had no choice but to stay as well. We sat as far in the back as possible because of my level of anxiety and anger. For this night the scheduled preacher did not show up, so they decided to have a time of testimony. Anyone could get up and say anything they wanted as long as it was related to God. By this time, I am realizing that the attitude in my heart is really rotten. I looked around the room and realized that I pretty much hated everyone there except my father. I felt superior in my education and in every other way that came to mind. This really bothered me, and I began to realize that something was seriously wrong with me. If I had learned anything from my grandfather, it was that Christians love people, not hate them.

An old man got up in the front of the room of about thirty people and began to talk about how he had been walking with God and had drifted away and wanted someone to come up and pray for him. He had one brown tooth and was dressed in rags. I looked at him in disgust and said to myself, "What could you possibly know about God?" I hated him. This really scared me. If I was a Christian, I would love him. For the first time it really hit me: *I am not Christian!* I was so upset that I was almost shaking. I was sitting between my father and one of the cleaned up street people. The mission worker got up and went forward to pray for the old man. I was panicking and hoping Dad would not go up also and leave me alone. He did. I knew that I did not know Jesus like my father, the men on Saturday morning, and even these cleaned up street people. They had something I did not have, which is probably why I hated them. I did not know how to get it. I was scared to death. I did not know what to say to Jesus. I knew it had something to do with knowing Him. There, alone in the back of the room, I bowed my head and finally said, "Lord Jesus, I want to know you."

After my prayer to Jesus I looked up and around the room. My father and the mission worker came back and sat down. I was expecting some kind of emotional rush or manifestation of God's acceptance of me, but there was nothing. A blind man got up to sing a solo and the man accompanying him on the piano was also blind. As he started to sing the song "Living for Jesus," I was entranced and captivated. The music was ethereal. An overwhelming desire came over me to get up and sing the song with the blind man. It was irresistible. Half way through the first verse I turned to my father and said, "I don't know why but I have to get up and sing this song with him." He said, "Well get up." I stood up. The singer could not see me so I had to interrupt him and ask him if I could sing the song with him. He and the piano player stopped and invited me to join them. We started the song again, and I sang alto. As I was singing, I looked around the room, and especially at the old man with the brown tooth. He was staring straight at me and our eyes met. I realized that I loved him. The hatred was gone. I quickly looked around the room at all the other people I had hated just a few minutes before. I loved them too. By this time, I was crying and tears were streaming down my face as I finished the song. Something had happened.

New Life

The first few days after that fateful Friday evening, I was delighted and confused: Delighted because I knew something fundamental and deep was different about me. I saw myself and everything around me in a new way. Confused because I did not know what had happened. The youth group I led at church could see it too. They wanted me to tell them how to have the new joy that seemed to bubble out of me. I could not tell them. All I knew was that it had something to do with knowing Jesus. Those first few weeks as a real Christian, I was in a kind of daze. I did not understand the scriptures about salvation in Christ Jesus even though I had read the Bible for years (II Corinthians 5:17).

I started attending the Friday night service at the Rescue Mission every week just like my father. At one of the services I met a man from the town where I went to college. He told me about their church and it was near where I lived. The following Wednesday evening I walked in the door for the midweek meeting. A young girl welcomed me along with others, and I had my first meeting in a church were most of the members really knew Jesus personally as Lord and Savior (John 17:3). The young girl was fifteen in late April of 1966, and I was twenty-two. She was a sophomore in high school, and I was a senior in college. Yes, she was my future wife, but neither of us had any thought of dating. To me she was one of the young people of the church, with emphasis on *young*. In time she saw me as a big brother. I would tease her how I wished I were younger or she was older so we could date. She would blush, and I was not embarrassed because I had no interest in dating her. I did think she was one of the prettiest girls I had ever met.

I continued to work in the laboratory at the hospital for the research psychologists. A few months after I asked Jesus to let me know Him, my boss got in some new tests to evaluate his patients. He wanted to use me as a practice patient to give him experience with the evaluation. I was hesitant because these were the same kind of tests the school psychologist had given me two years before that had indicated free floating anxiety.

My new boss did not know anything about my past, and I was afraid that the tests would reveal the same problem as the previous test with the school psychologist. It seemed that I was not worrying as much as before, so I decided to go ahead and let him give me the tests. The result was that I was completely normal, a result he expected but surprised me. I did not realize the depth of the change that had happened to me. In the first three months after that initial Friday night at the mission I had gained over twenty pounds. The anxiety over my health was gone. No more hypochondria or panic attacks. When I was tempted to worry, I would say to myself, "If I die, I die." Now that I knew Jesus, I also knew that I was going to Heaven if I died (I Thessalonians 4:13–18). In three months my anxiety over my health had completely gone away—the fear that had controlled me for at least eight years.

At my new church I quickly learned what had happened to me: I had been "born again" by receiving Jesus Christ as the sacrifice for my sins on the cross (John 3:1–21). With all my religious training it had never been clear to me why Jesus had to die on the cross or, more importantly, that He had died for me personally. I had understood it theologically but not as a living, life-transforming reality. When I sincerely said, "Lord Jesus, I want to know You," I did not realize, even at the time, what that really meant. All I knew at that moment was that I was weak, scared and needed help, and I was coming to Jesus to help me. It is a little like saying "I do" in a marriage ceremony. You say the words, you mean the words, but it takes a lifetime to experience the depth and richness of what saying those two simple words really involves. Similarly, when I told Jesus I acknowledged His Lordship and I wanted to Know Him, I did not realize that would initiate a living, real relationship with the Creator, God Himself.

This is why He created me and all human beings: to know Him, personally, *even intimately* (Acts 17:24–28). I did not know that the Holy Spirit is given as gift to live in the heart of the repentant sinner who comes to Jesus in humility and brokenness

(Romans 8:9–11). I knew I was very different, and the changes seemed to be deep down in me in a place even deeper than my fears. I realized I was different, and others saw it also. It was because I had been given a new life. The very life of Jesus Himself now somehow occupied my being (Colossians 3:1–4). Even now, over fifty years after that fateful night at the Nashville Rescue Mission, I don't understand how this mystery works: "Christ in me, Christ my life." I have learned that I don't have to understand it to enjoy it. That is the way love works, and the love of God the Father in Jesus Christ is the Ultimate Love (John 15:13).

The Scriptures I had read for years started to make sense. I learned the well-known salvation verses and also memorized many other verses. The Bible became a new book to me. It was almost like I had never read it. I was so excited about what Jesus had done for me I started telling everyone I met about Jesus and His love. I was privileged to see many lives changed those first few years as a real Christian. I say *real* because I had always thought I was a Christian. I learned that knowing Jesus personally is what makes a real Christian—not just knowing about Him theologically as I and my Dad and Mom had before (Matthew 7:15–23; John 17:3).

Through various circumstances I decided to continue at the same college and study for my master's in chemistry. It was a two-year thesis master's. In the second year, early spring 1968, I was part of a significant revival that occurred on campus. Our group went from nonexistent to being the largest spiritually-oriented group on campus. We did not even have a name. Every day Monday through Friday at 5:00 pm we would meet in a large classroom. Usually fifty to seventy would attend. Most of the meeting would be new Christians sharing how they came to know Jesus the day before. Prayer groups were started in almost every dorm on campus. Many of the administration heard the message of Jesus and His love, including the president of the university. No one knows how many students came to a saving knowledge of Jesus in the spring of 1968.

The Wind That Never Changes

During that time, I picked up a student who was hitchhiking back to the campus. In the five minutes he was in the car I told him about Jesus. Two weeks later one of the ladies in our church who worked with a statewide ministry for children asked me if I had picked up a hitchhiker on a certain date. One of her friends in another city had gotten a call from her son. It seems someone had given him a short ride and told him about Jesus. His mother had been praying for years that he would come to a real knowledge of Jesus. He had called his mom shortly after I had let him out of the car. He said, "Mom, I see what you have been trying to tell me all these years." I told my friend, "Yes, I was the one who picked him up and witnessed to him." This is just one of many remarkable things that happened during the revival on campus.

Because of all the excitement over what was going on at the university, a certain high school senior started coming to the 5:00 meetings. You can guess who that was. She was seventeen and about ready to graduate from high school. About this time in the spring of 1968, after a Sunday church service, her grandparents invited my parents and me to have lunch with them at the country club. They invited their seventeen-year-old granddaughter along as a social gesture to keep me company during lunch. I am sure they had no thought of encouraging any relationship between us. As I sat across the table from her I said to myself, "She is the prettiest girl I have ever seen." I asked her grandfather's permission to take her home after lunch. It was a warm spring day, so we stopped by a creek and walked over a suspension bridge. She hardly talked at all, and I was a chatterbox. I took her home and decided she is just too young.

Two months later she had graduated from high school and returned from a trip to Florida. I remember seeing her walk into the back of the church for the Sunday evening service. She looked so cute—all tan in her sleeveless dress. I decided to ask her out again. Same thing again—she hardly talked and I was a chatterbox. Again I decided she is just too young. I don't know why, but a few weeks later I asked her out a third time. This time she was no different, but something happened to me. I do not remember what we did, where we went, or anything about that date. All I know is that I took her home wildly in love with her. I was consumed.

Never before had I felt like this. I dated a lot in high school and college. I would always ask my mom what it would be like when I fell in love. She would just say, "You'll know." Well I did. That date happened in June of 1968, and the way I felt when I took her home is as vivid as if it happened yesterday. Looking back, the best way I could describe the difference with her was it was not about me. All my previous dating relationships were about how it made me feel or satisfied something in me. This time, all I could think about was how I could make her happy and please her. I fantasized how joyful it would be to have the privilege of taking care of her for the rest of her life.

My memory of the summer of 1968 is dominated with how much I thought about a certain young, beautiful girl. In time she started to talk a little. She wanted a big brother. While we went on dates, she considered them as being together as friends. That did not suit me at all. As I said earlier, I am a chatterbox, one of those people who are an open book. I could never be good at poker or anything that required hiding feelings. Amazingly, I never told her how I felt about her. This is totally uncharacteristic. I spill my guts instinctively. Somehow, that first summer I was as cool as she was on the outside. I wanted to be with her constantly. However, I wanted God's will even more. I was so scared of marrying the wrong person that I did not date her without much prayer. I would pray for confirming signs like asking God to let her answer the phone when I would call to ask her out. If someone else in the family answered the phone, I would not ask her out, and I was deeply disappointed. We dated all that summer and always had a good time together.

She and her parents had decided that she should go to college at a small Bible school near Chicago. This was about eight hundred miles away from where I was going to school. I did not agree with this at all. I prayed much that she would go to school where I was going. I only talked to God about this, never to her or anyone else. At this point she liked me but did not love me. I loved her desperately. For the first time in my life, someone else's happiness meant more to me than my own. I even prayed to God, "If marrying me is not best for her, then I don't want to marry her." I meant it. In August of 1968, as time drew close for her to leave for college, the acceptance letter that should have come in March or April had not come. In 1968 you did not just pick up the phone and call the school like today. I don't know why, but her parents never pursued finding out why the acceptance letter never arrived. After much prayer, she and her parents decided that she should go to the college in her town. She asked me to help her with the schedule. She signed up for the strongest academic courses, which included general chemistry. As a graduate student, one of my jobs was to teach general chemistry laboratories. She wound up in a laboratory section I was teaching. When I tell people she was in one of my lab sections they invariably accuse me of making that happen. Jesus knows I did not. I believe it was His doing.

I should mention that my two-year master's had gone into an extra summer and fall semester. My graduation was originally scheduled for May 1968. My research had not worked out, so I had to take an extra summer and fall and start all over with another approach to my master's thesis. The fall of 1968 is when we were in school together and she was in my laboratory class. So it seems I was there in the fall of 1968 because my research had not worked out. She was there in the fall of 1968 because it had not worked out for her to attend the college near Chicago. Later that fall we learned that the acceptance letter indeed had been mailed in March. It arrived in October. It had been lost in the mail for seven months. We continued to date that fall, and she fell in love with me. By Christmas we were talking about marriage.

I graduated in January of 1969, earning a master's in chemistry and also a commission as a Second Lieutenant in the Army. During my two-year graduate school I had also been enrolled in advanced ROTC as a graduate student. It was the only factor that kept me from being drafted out of graduate school into the Army during the Viet Nam conflict. One of my good friends in graduate school was drafted in his second year as I would have been had I not been in advanced ROTC.

Immediately after graduation I went into the Army as a Second Lieutenant in the Signal Corps. It was a two-year commitment that probably meant my second year would be a tour in Viet Nam. I did not want to marry her and then leave her for a year, so we decided to get married after I got out of the Army. During my first year I had assignments on the East Coast, with my final six months at Fort Knox, Kentucky. This location was only 175 miles from where my future wife lived. So, I spent almost every weekend with her those six months. I would leave her house around 2:00 on Monday morning and arrive back at Fort Knox between 4:00 and 5:00 am. You look back on things you did in younger years and wonder why you did them. By the way, her parents would always go to bed around 10:00 pm, so they never knew I was keeping their daughter up so late. Or, if they did know, they never said anything.

In September of 1969 I received my orders for my second year. It was a tour in Germany, not Viet Nam. Stunned and delighted, I called her and said, "Let's get married and go live in Germany for a year." She said yes. It is a family joke that I never actually asked her to marry me. I just assumed she would. Suddenly my future in-laws were faced with the task of putting together a large, formal wedding in less than four months. She was so young her mother had to accompany us to the County Clerk's office to give official permission for me to marry her. To this day I don't understand why her parents let me take their little nineteen-year-old girl out of college halfway through her sophomore year to go to Germany as my wife.

Our time in Germany together that first year was wonderful and sad: wonderful because we were married and able to travel and experience a different culture; sad, because the beginning of conflict started to be manifested in our relationship. It was a conflict caused by my weaknesses and insecurity.

I take most of the responsibility for the pain in our relationship. We were both "messed up," but I more. Remember my young introduction to pornography? It had never gone away, but just deepened into the bondage of sexual addiction and self-gratification. I had struggled with self-gratification since I was twelve years old. Becoming a real Christian did not take it away, nor did being married. God healed me of crippling anxiety and panic attacks when He saved me, but not this one. In marriage this all became known to my wife, and it broke her heart. It exacerbated her insecurities as a woman. At that time, I had a bad case of "wandering eyes," and after we were married she began to notice. As I write this it makes me sad to remember how I was in those days, but it is a necessary part of the story.

We fought constantly that first year. I discovered that I was very manipulative, especially in an argument. Unfortunately, I was good at turning things around and making it look like it was her fault. Sometimes it was her fault, but most of the time it was I who was in the wrong.

Although my wife was nineteen when I married her, she was unusually mature in some ways. After a particularly bad fight she had taken me back to work, and we were both still angry. We had been married about six months at this time. As she sat in the parking lot after I went into the building she asked herself, "What have I gotten myself into?" It was a good question. I was a selfish, immature jerk. As she sat there for a few minutes pondering the situation and what she should do, she finally decided, "We are going to make this work." I have told her many times over the years that I consider that decision one of the most mature and bravest decisions she has ever made. We managed to get through that first year. One good experience of that year was that we learned to work out our problems ourselves. No other family members were around to go to for help.

It is said that U.S. service personnel assigned to Germany come home with three things: a baby, a Volkswagen, and a cuckoo clock. We were two out of three. I went back years later on a business trip and bought a cuckoo clock.

After I got out of the Army, we both went back to college where she finished her last two years and graduated with her bachelor's, and I decided to go back to school for my Ph.D. in electrical engineering. I applied to several schools and was accepted at a university in the town where my parents lived and only thirty miles from my wife's parents.

For the next few years life was a blur. My wife was accepted into the same university where I was in graduate school and finished her B.A. degree. We were both in school full time for two years. Our first child was one year old when my wife went back to school, and she was pregnant with our second child when she graduated. For my last two years in graduate school she was in a small apartment with two young children while her husband studied and did his research about sixty to seventy hours a week. We had no married life. Life was school for me and kids for her. The fighting was less, but the fundamental problems of my sexual addiction and her insecurities were not any better. I received my degree and was offered a job in research and development in upstate New York. In January of 1976 we left our childhood homes for a new chapter in our lives.

Revelations

All my life I had worked, from being a paperboy at twelve to selling shoes in high school, and whatever had to be done to work my way through college and graduate school. The job in the hospital research laboratory had been my first professional position, but it was part time and did not pay a lot. Now, at last, I had a real job making real money—a Ph.D. electrical engineer in a major international high tech company doing research and development.

As I mentioned earlier, I was insecure in marrying into my wife's family, where everyone seemed important and wealthy. I wanted to prove to myself and others that I was worthy to be my wife's husband. I wanted to be somebody, to be significant.

The Wind That Never Changes

There were two ways I was going to pursue this goal: success in my secular profession and success in ministry. By this time my gifting in ministry had developed and I was a good Bible teacher. Over the past ten years as a real Christian I had attended four different churches. In each one I had been asked to teach Sunday school and Bible studies, and occasionally on Sunday mornings. My gifting as a speaker had been recognized in all these places and confirmed by my listeners. I am ashamed to say it, but I thought I was a spiritual hotshot who knew a lot about the Bible. In other words, I was very proud and insecure. My role as a Bible teacher made no contribution to my marriage. In fact, it was a detriment to my marriage.

It seems odd how I could be so smug about my Bible knowledge and yet still be in bondage to sexual addiction and self-gratification. Yet this is how it was. My life was a lie. To others I seemed knowledgeable, and I loved to impress them with how much I thought I knew (I Corinthians 8:2). In reality, I hated myself so much I would not let another person get close to me. I avoided close friendships with other Christian men because I did not what them to find out how messed up I was on the inside. I would use my Bible knowledge and communication skills to hold them at arm's length emotionally and was never real and open with anyone. I knew if they found how what I was really like they would not like me, so I kept up the façade. Only my wife really knew me. She would sit in the audience listening to me teach and see others be impressed with me and compliment my knowledge and teaching skill. What a mess!

You see, my wife did not like my teaching. It was not that the teaching was bad. As she told me later, my life did not match my teaching. I taught the truth, but I did not live it. The moment she told me this is vivid in my memory. I was sitting in a red recliner in our living room in upstate N. Y. We were having an argument about my teaching when she spoke those words to me. It was like a knife pierced a boil in my heart, and the poison came out. Strangely, it hurt and felt good at the same time. I didn't want to admit it, even to myself, but she was right. I was beginning to wake up as to what was really going on in my heart.

This was the pattern of our first few years of suburban life. My clear priorities were job and ministry, followed by everything else. In time I was used in our local church as a teacher and from the pulpit on Sundays when the pastor was out of town. This was typical. I also had a lot of ministry during the week. I taught Bible studies and did counseling, all for the glory of God, or so I thought. Now I know it was for the glory of me. Of course when you teach and speak God's Word good things happen. That does not mean, however, that you are doing what He really wants you to do. By day I lived for success at work. By night and weekends I lived for validation in Christian ministry. I could not understand why my wife was not excited when I would come home and tell her all the wonderful things God was doing through me. I would be out one or two nights a week while she was home with two small children. Sadly, I did not realize what I was doing to my beloved wife and children.

I should also mention that my role as Bible teacher and occasional counselor put me in contact with hurting women. My personality tended to attract such women who were divorced or in sad relationships. There was nothing improper from my part, but for some reason such women wanted to emotionally bond with me. At the time I did not realize how dangerous that was, but my wife did. She could not deal with other women seeking an emotional bond with her husband, especially when he was falling far short of having a right relationship with her. This was the final straw that made her want to leave me.

This phony lifestyle came to a climax about two years after I started the new job. My wife was pregnant with our third child. One morning, as she was getting ready, she was planning the final details on how she was going to leave me and our two daughters. She had decided that she would leave the two girls with friends for the day, and then not be there when I got home. As she pondered these events, God spoke to her: "You can't do that." She finished getting ready and called me at work. She

The Wind That Never Changes

wanted to go to dinner that night. At our favorite restaurant she told me everything. I was surprised to find out how much sorrow I had caused her in my devotion to ministry. Even then, I did not realize the depth of her pain. I didn't know it, but I had a lot to learn.

Strange as it may seem, her revelation about planning to leave me and the girls did not change things much. I was shocked and relieved, but not enough to change anything. Our third child was born, and my wife had severe post-partum depression. I would come home to dirty dishes from breakfast and lunch and no dinner fixed. She cried most of the time. I would wash the dishes, fix dinner, put the kids to bed, clean the house, and whatever else had to be done. Nighttime ministry was on hold for a while. This went on for about three months. Finally, we had it out in the basement one night after I had put everyone to bed. I told her we were going to do two things: go to counseling together and have some lady help her with the house work. She liked the first idea, but absolutely did not like the second. The idea of some woman coming into her house and helping with the cleaning increased her insecurity. She got up to leave, and I physically grabbed her by the shoulders and sat her back down. I am thankful to say this is the only time I have been physical with my wife. She still did not like the idea, but I was determined. The lady who came to help with housework was a wonderful, Godly woman raising four sons alone after her husband left her. She became like a spiritual mother to my wife and was a gift from God to both of us.

We found a Christian counselor and started going for one-hour sessions each week. The first two sessions were a time for the counselor to get to know us and our struggles together. The third week he looked me straight in the eye and announced that our problems were my fault. "What?" I thought! I am a wonderful husband and father. I wash dishes, change dirty diapers, work hard, provide for my family, and am faithful. Well, sort of faithful. How could her problems be my fault? The counselor shattered my self-righteous delusions with one insightful statement: "You are not meeting the emotional needs of your wife." He pointed out that my helping her was hurting our relationship because my attitude was, "Because you can't do this, I will do it for you." I should be coming alongside her as a partner and encourager. My superior, condescending attitude was just driving her further into depression.

As unsettling as this was, it got a lot worse. The counselor told me that I needed to stop all ministries and learn to love my wife. Stop all ministries! That is like asking a concert pianist to give up the piano. Christian ministry was my life, my identity, my self-worth! Ministry gave me significance, importance, and validation, perhaps even more so than my job. Of all the things the counselor said that day, this was the one I could not receive.

We continued to go each week to the sessions. The counselor would not back off from his recommendations, and I would not budge on giving up ministry. My wife wisely did not push me but let me and the counselor fight it out. During lunch break at work I decided to take a long walk and talk to the Lord Jesus about all this. I said, "Lord, You have given me the gift of teaching Your Word and many opportunities to use that gift. Why did you give me a wife that could not support my gift?"

Immediately after I asked the Lord why, I received an answer: "The things in your wife that you consider stumbling blocks are, in reality, stepping stones to bring you to Me." I heard those words as clearly as if someone were walking beside me and spoke them.

I cannot explain what it is like to hear God's voice directly like this. Over the years He has spoken directly to me many times. Typically, it is out of the blue and not something I was thinking or doing at the time.

Of all the times He has spoken to me, this one stands out in my memory as the clearest. As He spoke to me, He also opened my understanding with a revelation on marriage. I suddenly understood that in a Godly marriage, the wife's weaknesses are for perfecting the husband, and the husband's weaknesses are for perfecting the wife. My wife's weaknesses develop and ma-

The Wind That Never Changes

ture the fruit of the Spirit in me.

In later years I realized that this principle works in all Christian relationships. It is easier to be a Christian loner and not have anything to do with God's people. I have heard of people saying, "I am very spiritual." My question would be, "With whom?" I have learned that real spirituality is learning to forgive, love, and serve all God's people and also the unsaved, warts and all. Everyone has "warts." One of the best words of wisdom I heard as a young Christian is, "Nobody has it together." It is part of the exercise as a real Christian to learn to love and serve imperfect people (Luke 15:2).

Suddenly, it seemed as if I were walking three feet off the ground. My Heavenly Father wanted me to know Him better. He wanted me to draw near to Him. He was using my wife's weaknesses to accomplish what I wanted more even than teaching —to be closer to Him. This all happened in the middle of a large parking lot in less than one minute. I don't know how God can reveal so much in so little time with such life-changing implications, but He did. My first reaction was to find a phone booth. Remember, this was in 1978. I was so excited to call my beloved wife and tell her what God had told me. I told her briefly, and also to get a baby sitter because we were going out to dinner. That evening, again at our favorite restaurant and our favorite table, I told her I was going to give up all ministries. As time went on with my new insight, I also realized that along with Christian ministry, my job and career had been a higher priority than my wife and family and a higher priority than even Jesus Himself. Because of the insecurity in my heart, I had been looking to success in ministry and my job to prove I was a worthy person.

A new goal was birthed in my heart. I told my wife, "My goal is for you to know that the only thing in my heart that is higher than my love for you is my personal love for the Lord Jesus." That goal morphed into a little statement that I have said to her ever since, "After Jesus, you're number one."

While God's revelation to me regarding my relationship to

my wife and Him was life changing and put us, especially me, into a new and better direction, my struggles with my sexual addiction were still with us. Perhaps for this reason my wife's depression was not as debilitating, but still there. She came to the conclusion that our present church was too focused on ritual and not really meeting her need for more teaching on living in the power of the Holy Spirit (Ephesians 3:14–21). She wanted to try another church we had heard about that emphasized a deeper daily walk with our Lord Jesus. Our counselor attended that church, and also a close friend of mine at work who I respected greatly.

We started attending that church and were introduced to workings of the Holy Spirit that we were not used to—in particular, the filling of the Holy Spirit (Ephesians 5:15–21). This is a controversial topic among committed Christians. Two good books on the subject are *They Speak with Other Tongues* by John Sherrill and *Baptized in the Spirit* by Randy Clark.

After about a year at that church, we both were slowly opening up to things that were new for us. My wife was sharing about her battle with depression at a Bible study. The others in the study, all long-time members of our new church, said that they wanted to pray that my wife would be filled with the Holy Spirit. She sat on some stairs and everyone gathered around and prayed for her to be filled with the Holy Spirit. I just watched. She confesses that she did not notice anything different that evening. However, the next morning she discovered that the depression was gone. This depression had kept her miserable ever since we had moved to upstate New York, at this time about four years. Now it was just gone. It stayed gone.

With my wife's depression gone and my priorities adjusted, it would seem that everything was going well. While it was much better, there was still the sexual addiction in my life that was a constant source of pain and conflict for both of us. Over the years I had tried everything I could think of to deal with my weakness with pornography and giving in to self-gratification. There was no internet, but it was always easily available. Some-

The Wind That Never Changes

one at work had it, and I always knew where it was located. Unfortunately, my memory was full of enough input to constantly plague me even if I never saw another sad image.

The breakthrough came about a year after my wife was healed of depression. A special speaker was at our new church, and a meeting was scheduled for Friday evening. I really did not want to go and was looking for an easy excuse. Just after dinner, I asked my wife if she was tired and wanted me to stay in that evening and not go to the meeting. Surprisingly, she strongly encouraged me to go. This did not please me. For some reason I was somewhat afraid to go, similar to that first night at the rescue mission when my father made me go with him.

With no excuse not to go, and my wife's strong encouragement to go, I went to the meeting. I sat as far in the back as I could. The church was full, at least three hundred people. By this time we had been attending this Church for two years. While not doing any official ministry, I occasionally got up to share a word of exhortation on Sunday mornings during a time set aside for anyone to share. My gifting in the Word usually came through, and the congregation had learned to enjoy it when I shared. It also meant that everyone knew me.

The guest speaker got up to share and said something that stunned us. "Tonight the Lord wants to deliver men who have a problem with sexual addiction. If you want to be delivered, come down front for prayer." We all sat there in silence, waiting. No one moved. The speaker said something else I don't remember, along the lines of why men needed to come forward. He wanted me and men like me to get up in front of all these people—men, women, children—and admit publicly a deep, horrible weakness. Finally, a man on the front row got up and walked about ten feet to the prayer rail. I would not get off so easy. I was in the back of the church. This was not one of those times where everyone is standing up and singing and you can kind of sneak up front. Everyone was still seated, and by now we had been waiting for about five minutes, which seemed like an eternity. I struggled with my pride and what everyone would think of me, the great, gifted Bible teacher.

I decided that I hated this sin in my life so much, I didn't care what anyone thought of me if there was a chance I could be free. Getting up out of my seat, I slowly walked forward with what felt like every eye in the place on me. I thought I heard some murmurs or something like gasps as I walked up. I died what seemed a thousand deaths before I got to that prayer rail. My pride was devastated. I didn't care. If wounded pride was the price I had to pay, so be it. I know that nothing I do can add to the finished work of Jesus on the cross. However, I also know that pride is one of the biggest barriers we have to God's working His grace into our lives, and I had a big dose (James 4:6).

I knelt down at the prayer rail, and the speaker prayed a simple prayer. That was it. Only two of us went forward that evening. Knowing what I do about Christian men, a lot more should have gone forward.

The first thing that changed after that fateful night was recognizing the influence of visual input on my thought life. Television, even in 1981, had a lot of sexual content. I learned that it was easier to have a pure thought life if I watched less television (Ephesians 5:11). Also, there was a new desire to please my Heavenly Father and not look at things or think thoughts that would lead to lustful feelings. This desire had been in my heart since I had asked Jesus to let me know Him, but now it seemed stronger, more compelling. It says in Ephesians 3:16 that we should pray "that God would grant you, according to the riches of His glory, to be strengthened with power through His Spirit in the inner man." This is the primary thing that was different. Somehow, someway I had a greater desire to obey God and do His will and the power to do it. All I can say is, "Thank you Lord." Many things have happened to me that I cannot understand or explain since I asked Jesus to let me know Him. This is just one of them.

With my new desire and power, I continued to make good choices. Over time the choices became easier. I cannot say sexual temptation has completely gone away, even forty years later. I still have to choose to obey my God to continue to enjoy His freedom. The flesh is still in me, and it has not improved. Its influence is much weaker as I grow in the grace and knowledge of God (II Peter 3:18).

It is like a story I heard as a young Christian: An old believer was commenting about two dogs fighting is his heart. One was good, the other was bad. Someone asked him which one was winning. He said, "The one I feed" (Acts 2:42).

Now I can truly say that sexual lust getting control of my heart is the rare exception instead of the dominating rule, as it was prior to that Friday night. After my Lord Jesus delivered me I can look anyone in the eye and say, "God can deliver you from all sin." We will never achieve sinless perfection in this life. However, the power of God can and will bring us to a place where sin is the exception and victory in Jesus is the rule. As I write this chapter it has been over thirty-five years since I gave in to self-gratification. To God be the glory!

With my priorities adjusted and the great weakness of my heart healed, I was ready for the next step in my growth. I had no idea that God was just getting started.

Death to Self

A new job meant relocation of the family to another city. By this time we had four children, and left the address where we had lived for six years. Those six years were perhaps the saddest years of our marriage as God had begun to adjust my insecurity-driven priorities and delivered me from a great sin in my life. At this point I had been out of Christian ministry for three years and was continuing to learn how to love my wife. I had also been free from my sexual addiction for two years. One would think that my understanding of how to be a good husband and father was coming along well. It was, and my wife was happier, but many changes were on the horizon. In hindsight, I know what was going on, but I did not know it at the time. God was tearing down my life.

For my first sixteen years as a real Christian, I really did not understand the implications of the Lordship of Christ in my everyday living. I was about to learn. Up to this time God was working on major foundation problems. Now, He was starting to work on the structure that everyone sees, including my family. He was about to shake me to the core again with more foundation work, and finally rebuilding my life in a way that would glorify Him and not me. He taught me through humility lessons, being-thankful-when-I-did-not-want-to-be-thankful lessons, and submission lessons.

In our new church I was to learn that Bible knowledge was not the goal. The pastor said to me one day, "You know the Bible better than any of us." However, all the leadership knew Jesus better than I. That was what I was here to learn.

The new church was similar to our previous church in that it emphasized walking in the Holy Spirit but was a little different in its approach to training new members. After getting to know us as a family and me as a potential leader, one of the elders was assigned to mentor me personally. I had met this man previously when he had visited our last church and was immediately impressed with his gentleness, wisdom, and knowledge of Jesus. I asked him how he became so sweet. He said with a twinkle in his eye, "The many years Jesus has used a 2 X 4 to get my attention and straighten me out." After a few months in our new church this man and his wife became mentors to my wife and me.

I was not sure I liked this arrangement. Frankly, I did not think I needed a mentor. At thirty-eight I had been a real Christian for sixteen years, married for twelve years, had four children, was very successful in my career as a research engineer, and now a new manager of advanced technology with Ph.D.'s reporting to me. In other words, I was still proud. My pride had been wounded, but not enough to render it secondary in my heart with regard to how I saw myself. Pride can never be completely eradicated, but it can come under the authority of

Jesus and be minimal in the sense of controlling responses and decisions. A. W. Tozer said, "Pride is the stubbornest root that grows in the heart of man." As I said earlier, pride is the biggest hindrance to experiencing the grace of God. "God resists the proud but gives grace to the humble" (James 4:6). I was about to enter more advanced lessons in humility. Such lessons are never pleasant.

Humility

My mentor's first observations are as follows: "You are not much of a husband or a father. Your children's obedience is not crisp." He spoke those very words looking me straight in the eye. My initial reaction was indignation. It was so hard to hear those words. Who was he to say such things to me? Still, I could not deny the presence of Jesus in this man. I decided to submit to him as unto the Lord. It was not easy. I thought I knew more than others. He was patient as he continued to say things that were very hard to hear. We spent hours together on Saturdays doing tasks for people in the church. As we worked together he dug deeper into my heart to find out what made me tick. After two months he came up with a word that made the previous exhortations look like spiritual kindergarten.

He looked me in the eye and said, "You must forget everything you think you know about the Bible." This word was as hard for me to hear as the counselor's word on quitting all Christian ministries—even harder. I could not believe what he was saying! I did not realize that my Bible knowledge was a god in my heart, but my mentor did. It was a god that would keep me back from knowing the real God better. It was a god that fed my self-image, my false identity. I thought my Bible knowledge was a major component of my relationship with Jesus. I had not learned yet that the Bible is a means, not the end (John 5:39, II Timothy 3:15). *Knowing Jesus is the end* (Philippians 3:8–10). My mentor did not mean that I was to actually forget all that I had learned about the Bible, but to not let it be my god. At first I could not see the difference, but then God got in on the act by giving me two visions.

To me it is amazing that God loves us so much that He wants to take us to new heights of knowing and loving Him. All of these events were ordained by Him: getting a new job, going to a new church, having a mentor, and finally zeroing in on a major problem. I wrestled with the latest word from my mentor. By this time, I had grown to really love and respect him, but I could not understand what he was getting at by telling me to not consider as important my knowledge of the Bible. I even lost sleep over this one because I could not understand why it was so important.

One afternoon I was sitting on my couch in the living room and pondering these things about two weeks after my mentor had spoken them to me. Strangely, suddenly I vividly saw a cat in a tree. The best way I can describe it is a hologram, like a movie in thin air. As I looked closer at the scene in front of me, I saw that the cat was hanging on for dear life and the tree was being violently shaken. The longer I watched, the tree was being shaken more and more, and the cat could hardly hold on. At that point the Lord spoke to me: "You are the cat, and the tree is your knowledge of the Bible. I am going to shake you out of the tree." He didn't tell me then what happens when the cat falls. I later learned that the cat falls into His arms. As Christians, in our humanity and ignorance of what it means to be a child of God, we try to tie ourselves to God with strings—strings of knowledge, tradition, good works, theology, religion and so forth. Until He starts cutting them, we do not realize that these strings that we so carefully guard are keeping us from a deeper knowledge of Him. Usually when He starts cutting the strings, we panic. We don't know that He is trying to teach us that all we have or need is Him. He wants us to learn to rest in His strong arms, not tie ourselves to Him with strings of our own making.

About a week later I was praying in my bedroom. Again, in front of me was a vision. This time I saw two people walking together. I could not see their faces, as the view was from behind them. The figure on the right was holding an ancient lantern in His right hand to light the way. I realized it was Jesus. The figure on the left was me, and we were holding hands, my right hand holding His left hand. My first thought was that this was a precious event walking along with Jesus. Then I realized that I was on His left. I was on the "goat side" (Matthew 25:31–46). I almost panicked. I raced through my Bible knowledge to see if it is ever alright to be on the left side of Jesus. As I went through my mental concordance, I remembered a verse: "Behold you hold me by my right hand" (Psalm 73:23). Whew, it is alright to be on His left hand!

You see, the point is that I could not accept a precious vision of Jesus and me together without first checking it with what I thought I knew about the Bible. His revelations of Himself to me were limited by my understanding of His Word. The Holy Spirit never does anything contrary to the Word of God; He often does things contrary to our understanding of the Word of God. He is not limited to our understanding. If we limit Him to our understanding, we will not make much progress in our walk with Him. A few days later I saw the vision again with a larger view. On the right side of Jesus was a sharp drop off. Being on His left had nothing to do with being on the "goat side." He was keeping me on the left to protect me. I was finally starting to get it.

By this time our new mentors had been spending about six months with us. One day they announced, "We do not need to meet together anymore." My wife and I were both shocked and disappointed. We had grown to love both of them. While I have not gone into any details about my wife's experiences with her mentor, they were similar to mine in that they were life-changing. Neither of us wanted to stop, and we tried to persuade them to continue. Their reply was, "You are both pointed in the right direction now. That is what we wanted to accomplish." Their goal for both of us was to learn to look unto Jesus instead of ourselves or each other (Hebrews 12:1–2). Prior to our time with our mentors we would have both absolutely confessed we were looking unto Jesus. Now that our Savior had done work in both our hearts, we realized we were just starting to learn how to look unto Jesus as He desires. Looking unto Jesus more and more is a lifetime exercise in growth.

We still felt very needy. Both of our mentors had spoken things to us that were very hard to hear, very humbling. Now that we had gotten used to being humbled and saw the fruit in our lives, we did not want to stop. This all happened twenty-eight years ago as I write this. My wife and I consider this couple as a spiritual father and mother. They were a precious gift from God.

Being Thankful

In our church I considered it a big deal to be a home group leader. Usually, an elder or an elder in training led a home group. I wanted to be a home group leader in the worst way. By this you can tell that I still had a long way to go. I equated being a home group leader to being a success in the church. I was very success-driven. So after two years I was up for consideration. Through various circumstances which were my fault, I was passed over, and a much younger, less experienced and less knowledgeable man was picked. I was devastated. How could they pick him! His children are much younger than mine, he does not have near the experience that I have, and, my favorite drum to beat, he does not know the Bible nearly as well as I do.

Of course, I was wrong again. The Lord wanted me to be thankful and embrace what was happening. He wanted me to even be happy that the other man was chosen instead of me. Eventually, I got there and was happy.

Submission

I didn't do very well in the submission department. My external response was correct, but my heart was not cooperating. I still struggled a little with that knowledge thing. The final test was our pastor, who spoke every Sunday. His teaching style was like someone swinging a machete. He made broad, sweeping statements about certain verses and applications that made my head spin. It got so bad that I went home almost every Sunday with a headache. I would get home and complain to my wife about this week's sermon and what was wrong with it. One day she said, "Will you stop bad-mouthing our pastor! I am tired of hearing about it. He ministers to me." Long story short, the Lord kept me in that situation until I learned to submit to the Pastor and appreciate him. By the time I left that church, we were good friends.

The final event in this stage of my training is one last vision. I had been through humility lessons, being-thankful-when-you-are-not-chosen-lessons, and submission lessons. This time the vision was a funeral parlor. I could just see into a room where there was a casket. As I looked closely, the person in the casket was me. Then the curtains closed, and the vision was over. I was a little worried. I said, "Lord, am I going to die." He replied, "No, the old you is dead." A short time later I became a home group leader and elder in that church. As I mentioned earlier, pride is never completely eradicated. However, the Holy Spirit can bring pride under the Lordship of Jesus to the degree that we can serve him without pride having dominion.

It is important to the security of the wife for her husband to be the spiritual leader of the home by setting the tone in Godliness. She wants to come under her husband's leadership and be confident he is seeking God with his whole heart. My wife wanted to submit to me as a woman of God, but I made it a lot more enjoyable by becoming a real man of God—a man she could follow and trust, and who would always point her to Jesus. The lessons I learned taught me to trust in Him in a way that I never had before. Over time my wife saw brokenness in me that allowed the life of Jesus to be more manifest. This made her more secure.

This was a major factor in her being free. Her husband was becoming a man of God who loved and desired to be holy as the highest priority of his life. Now, because of his love and knowledge of Jesus, he did not ever want to look at another woman improperly. He was doing this for his love of Jesus. She was able to enjoy the results. Her husband wanted her to be the most secure, loved, and radiant woman in the world. As I said earlier, my love for my wife and how to best love her grew in proportion to my love and knowledge of Jesus.

It had been a little over six years since I stopped all ministries to show my wife, "After Jesus, you are number one." I had learned from my mentor that my wife is my number one ministry—more important than my Christian service as a home group leader or elder, and certainly more important than my professional career. Now my priorities are Jesus, my wife, my children, and then everything else. I had been in leadership in our church for about a year, and this had marked my official start of ministry again after a five-year sabbatical. Now that I was living what I was teaching, my wife was my chief cheerleader. Now that we were one in Him, we had no idea what He had in mind.

Learning to Trust More

In the summer of 1986 I had started to teach again on Sunday mornings and also as a home group leader. This particular day I needed to make copies for the next home group meeting. I knew where the closest store was to make the copies, so I got in my car. For some reason I could not find the store. In some level of frustration and maybe a little stubbornness I said to myself, "I will find that store if I have to drive all the way to the center of town." I drove many blocks to the end of the street I was on and had to turn right. I knew the store was on the street I was on, but somehow I missed it. Because of one-way streets I had to take a circuitous route to get back to that street where I turned right so I could cruise it again and find the store. I slowly backtracked the street again until I came to a stop light near the end of the street. As I sat at the light waiting for green, there across the street was the store. How had I missed it before? At this point, out of the blue, God spoke to me: "All you have covered I have given to you." I mentally retraced the route I had taken. I said, "Lord that is the worst section of this town." It was full of drugs, empty buildings, graffiti, bars, prostitution, shootings, and homeless street people. We never went to that section of town. I tried to put this out of my mind. By this time I knew when God spoke to me. I knew it was Him, but I did not want to receive what He meant. That section of town scared me, and I wanted nothing to do with it.

I told my wife about what the Lord had said to me and tucked it away in my heart. It never really went away. It was on the back of my mind, and I was hoping He did not mean what I was afraid He meant.

A few months later I heard of a meeting for people interested in inner-city ministry. I was not really interested in this kind of ministry, but somehow I knew I was to attend this meeting. As I walked into the house, there were about a dozen people gathered that I did not know, nor did they know me. As we went around the circle introducing ourselves and why we were there, suddenly a man got up across the circle and came over to me. He stood behind me and put his hands on my shoulders. He said, "Thus says the Lord: 'I have called you to be the pastor of the inner-city. You are the pastor of the inner-city.'" He said this forcefully and loudly. Then he sat down. We all sat there in silence for a few minutes, then the others started to congratulate me on God's call on my life. I did not tell them about what God said to me at the stoplight a few months before. This was the first confirmation.

As time went on, I was beginning to realize that God wanted me to start an outreach evangelical ministry in the inner-city exactly where He had told me. By the spring of 1987 this burden was growing, but I was resisting. Our suburban church was right in the middle of a major building program. As an elder I was also very involved. I decided that this was a good time to bring up a new outreach ministry since they would all surely say that my focus should be on our building program. So one night at an elders meeting I proposed that our church sponsor an outreach ministry to the inner-city. Without exception, every one of my fellow elders and the pastor were excited and supportive. The pastor said he had been praying for this for years and was encouraging me to head up the outreach. This is not what I was expecting to hear or what I wanted to hear: the second confirmation.

A full year later I was still dragging my feet in responding to the call of God on my life. I was dragging my feet because I was afraid. My wife and children would be exposed to street people, drug addicts, alcoholics, the homeless, and everything else that goes along with inner city life. My wife and I had started talking about inner-city ministry, and she felt like I did. Neither of us wanted the stress of what this would mean to us and our four children. Our pastor strongly suggested my wife and I attend a leader's conference in North Carolina. I was amazed how easily everything fell in place for us to be away for a long weekend. In one of the sessions the Lord spoke to me and my wife powerfully—so much so, that we both agreed to spend the lunch break praying. She went back to our room, and I went out into the woods. I knew what the Lord wanted me to do. He knew I was afraid. I was afraid for myself, my wife, and my children. Since my early childhood, violent people scared me. I could resist no longer. Weeping on my knees alone in the woods, I told the Lord I would go to the inner-city, start an outreach, and eventually establish a church. As it turned out, at the same time, my wife made the exact same commitment to the Lord. We had not discussed what was on our hearts after that fateful session: third confirmation.

By now it was summer of 1988. I was still dragging my feet, but the burden was getting intense and compelling. One Sunday morning I was about to share a word with the congregation. As I was getting up out of my chair, the Lord spoke to me: "Obey Me or keep your mouth shut." There was anger in His voice. I had never heard that before. Those words hit me with such force it knocked me back in my seat, and I did not get up and share.

The Wind That Never Changes

Still dragging my feet because of fear, I did not start. About a month later I had a vivid dream that Jesus had returned, and I had not obeyed Him in starting the ministry that He called me to start. It was very real and I woke up almost in a sweat. It scared me that I would enter eternity not doing something He called me to do. Not that I would lose my salvation, but that I was certainly not a "good and faithful servant": forth confirmation.

Late in the summer of 1988 the final straw came in the form of a book that my cousin had sent me about the return of Christ. I had looked at it, and put it into a drawer and forgot it. This particular Sunday evening I picked it up and started reading. I found it compelling and convicting. All night I stayed up and read that book. I finished it about 6:00 am. My wife came in and found a somewhat wild-eyed husband who announced he was starting the inner-city ministry as soon as possible. She said, "Fine—do it."

That week I went to the office of a local businessman to ask permission to use his parking lot on Friday nights for street meetings. As I stood in the waiting room I could hear him say, "Who is it? What does he want? No, I don't have time to talk to him." As his secretary walked out of his office I was praying. I said to her, "Ask him for five minutes, just give me five minutes." She went back to tell him. I walked into his office. He was not in a good mood. I told him what I wanted to do in his parking lot on Friday nights. Finally, he looked at me and said, "At least you will keep the prostitutes away a few hours. Alright, get me a certificate of insurance to cover your activities. I don't want to be sued because of you."

It took another week to get the insurance, make an announcement at church, and organize our first Friday night session. The Lord touched the hearts of six others in the church to be with my wife and me. On the third Friday of September 1988, we started, with fear and trembling. We did not know what to do or how to do it. I just knew I had to start. It is ironic that God called me to reach out to street people. When I first came to know Jesus, I was with street people. Now, twenty-two years later, I had come full circle. The kind of people that I had hated that first fateful Friday night at the rescue mission in 1966, I was now seeking to reach for Jesus Christ and His love.

Fear was not my only problem in starting the inner-city ministry. A year before, I had realized that I could not be a manager and start a major enterprise outside of my job. Being a manager was very stressful and demanded a great deal of my energy. By this time, I was a second-line manager and had managers reporting to me. I went to my boss and told him I had to get out of management. I did not tell him why. He complied with my request and started the process to replace me at my second-line position. By the time I started the inner-city ministry, I was out of management completely and back to being an engineer. I thought my career was over.

You never know what is going to happen when you obey God with abandon. I had to obey Him whatever the cost. He knew I loved my job and wanted to be successful. For the first six months out of management I was lost and depressed at work. The story of how He blessed me as an engineer is almost as exciting as what was going to happen in my family and the inner-city ministry. In the end, He let me be promoted to the very executive level as an engineer as I would have been promoted as a manager. He did not allow my career to suffer for obeying Him. In fact, He blessed it beyond my wildest expectations. I retired as a Distinguished Engineer, an executive position equivalent to a Director level, with numerous awards and more U.S. Patents than I want to mention. At my retirement party years later, every person who spoke something about my career had something positive to say about my Christianity and how it had affected them to work with me; He was glorified.

For the next fifteen years my wife, children, and I were involved in inner-city ministry. It consumed our lives, but God gave us more grace. By 1991 we became a church, and I was the pastor. Several books could be written about what happened those fifteen years. We saw many supernatural workings of God

The Wind That Never Changes

and many lives changed. It seems that on the front line, God is willing to manifest Himself in ways that don't normally happen in a typical suburban church. C. T. Studd once said that he wanted a mission on the edge of hell. That was our church. If a pin was put in the city map for every shooting that occurred in the inner city of Poughkeepsie, NY, our church was in the middle of all the pins. One night someone was shot in front of the church, which was located in the "red light" district. We learned to love and minister to the unloved and outcasts.

About ten years into the ministry I was discouraged. We could not seem to grow beyond about thirty to forty members. People would come and hear the Word and be born again. People would be changed and healed over time, and then God would take them away to some other place or church. I complained to the Lord about this. He said, "Are they your sheep?" I said, "No, Lord." Even after His correcting me, I was still depressed. I decided to fast forty days and seek His face for what I was missing in this ministry.

For those forty days I drank only liquids. I had a smoothie at least once a day with eggs, a frozen banana and peanut butter. I was still working as a research and development engineer and had to keep up some energy. The rest of the time I had carrot juice or fruit juice. In those forty days I lost thirty pounds. During that time, I prayed fervently every day and asked the Lord what was I missing or how had I missed it? It was a sweet time of seeking Him, but He did not give me any answer.

About three weeks after the forty-day fast was over, a lady I had never seen before showed up at a Sunday morning service. She drove a car and had a big Bible. In this ministry we got excited when someone came who drove a car. This may have meant that she was not "spiritually bleeding all over the floor" as most of our visitors were when they first came in the door. During the message I noticed this new person listened very intently to what I was saying. I said in my heart, "She is surely a mature Christian."

After the service was over, the new person walked straight

up to me and asked me to get my wife. When my wife came over, the lady said she had a message from God for both of us. She explained that she had been praying and ministering to the Lord about a week before. As she was waiting on the Lord, He spoke to her a Word for a church in Poughkeepsie that had "Bread" in the church name. She said she did not know about any of the churches in Poughkeepsie so she called her daughter who lived there. Her daughter had been to our church before. She told her mother about Bread of Life, the address, and when we had our service on Sunday mornings.

Now here she was to tell us what the Lord had told her to say. The very first words of the message from the Lord were, "You have not missed it." She went on to tell us how the Lord had sent us there to minister to the ones that society had thrown away, and that we were doing exactly what He called us to do. This was an amazing encouragement from our Father. No one but my wife knew why I was seeking God those forty days. He knew, and spoke it to His servant who lived sixty miles away, someone who had never heard of Bread of Life church, much less the pastor and his wife. This cured me of worrying about how many members we had in the church.

For fifteen years I never got over the fear in my gut when I headed to the inner-city. Every time, the Spirit of God would manifest His glory and the fear would go away. I have been threatened with someone holding a brick, been intimidated by someone with a big knife, come close to being mugged, and had a convicted murderer sleeping in my basement. One of my favorite stories is the night one of my parishioners called me at 2:00 am to rescue him from a drug deal at the roughest bar in the county. I was too afraid to go by myself, so I called one of the elders to go with me. As I backed out of the driveway I put on the Christian radio station to strengthen me. What I heard was, "Let goods and kindred go, this mortal life also. The body they may kill. God's truth abides still." I said, "Thanks a lot, Lord." It got to the point that almost every time the phone rang, my heart would race. Stopping a fight between two convicted felons in the parking lot, going into drug houses where I could have been killed, and visiting parishioners and hearing gunshots outside were just part of the ministry. Through it all He protected us and revealed His love and power to redeem the helpless and hopeless.

The inner-city ministry was so demanding, so overwhelming, so scary that I had to learn to trust Jesus in a way that I never had before. I look back at those fifteen years when I worked as an engineer and pastored an inner-city church and wonder how we did it.

I don't know how my wife and I did it. But we did, and we did it together. This is a key point in this story. By this time my wife and I were more in unity than any time in our marriage. As we both focused on Jesus as our life and strength, we were being made one in a way we never could have imagined. When I stood up to teach on Sunday mornings I felt as if she were standing there beside me. A. W. Tozer said, "God's message is the man." My message was how Jesus changed me and made me into a man of God that my wife could love, honor, and follow. God can change any person into the image of Christ any way He chooses. In my case, He chose marriage.

The expressions of our lives individually were really an expression of our unity. When she ministered I was with her. We did nothing on our own individually, but as we both manifested Jesus, our oneness with each other increased so much others could see it. Many times over the years men and women have expressed interest in why we seem to be so close. We take no credit. Jesus did it all.

In His Presence

By the summer of 1999 we had been ministering in the inner-city for eleven years, and the last nine years as a church. I was working as an engineer, and by this time was learning how the Lord was blessing my job even though I had removed myself from management. One day at work a woman passed by me in the hall and greeted me by name. I should have known her name, but I am generally very bad at remembering names. I was again embarrassed that I did not remember her name. As she walked by I said hi and walked on a few steps. Then I stopped and asked her again what her name was. She said "Terry." "Of course," I said. "Terry." As I walked away I was thinking about what kind of association I could make of her name so I could remember her the next time. I made a mental picture of her praying and waiting on the Lord. "That's it: She tarries in the presence of the Lord." Now I will remember her the next time I see her. At that moment the Lord spoke to me: "You don't do that." My heart was smitten so much I started to cry. Like most Christians I had always struggled with having a consistent quiet time each day. It had always been hit and miss, mostly miss.

Yes, I was up to my ears in ministry, and yes, I was learning to love my wife, but I had been neglecting my personal time with Him. Right there in that hallway I committed to the Lord that the next morning I would give the first hour of my day to Him every day. Thus began a new phase in my continuing journey in becoming a man of God and learning to love my wife. To this day, over eleven years later, I still strive to keep that commitment. I must confess that events in my life for the past few months have made this more difficult, and I have been struggling to maintain my schedule. However, this very morning I spent time with Him from 6:00 to 7:00 am. Other than the most recent few months, I have kept that commitment with a clear conscience. After the first year of being in His presence every morning, my wife came to me and said that I had changed more in that year than any other time in our marriage.

I asked her some years later why she said that I had changed so much in that first year. She said it was hard to define. It seems that even my personality had changed. To her, I was becoming more like Jesus. The Apostle Paul said in I Corinthians 11:1, "Be imitators of me as I also am of Christ." Becoming like Jesus has never been an obvious or easy process. The thoughts I am sharing in this chapter are the closest I can come to explaining the process.

When I first became a home group leader and elder in 1985, I had decided to give the first two hours of my day to the Lord. I did this for about a year. My children still remember coming downstairs at 6:00 am and seeing the light on in the sitting room where I had my quiet time every morning. While this sounds good, I had not yet learned the significant role motive plays when we seek God. I was seeking Him to be a better leader. This is not wrong, but it is not best either.

God does not want us to seek Him because we want something. It is fine to ask for things and seek guidance, but these are not the primary reason for seeking Him. The result of my two hours every day was spiritual pride. I began to feel smug that I was spending so much time in prayer and the Word. It came to a climax one day when someone spoke in church about how we were not spending enough time with God. He challenged all of us to stand up and commit ourselves to spend more time in prayer. Everyone in the place stood up but me. I don't know what they all thought. They didn't know what I was doing. I finally stood up because I didn't want to look uncommitted. This got me to thinking. I realized it was pride that made me not want to stand up. I stopped the two hour every morning regime. After that it was back to hit and miss.

Now here I was again, thirteen years later, committing to a daily time with the Lord every morning for an hour. How was this going to be different? For the past nine years I had preached every Sunday and led a Bible study every Wednesday evening. Most of my time with the Lord had been several hours each week in preparation. He wanted more and wanted me to learn how to seek Him.

By this time in my walk with God I had learned that what He really wanted was me. Yes, he wanted me to serve Him, but that was secondary to seeking Him. He wants to be with me and reveal Himself to me. He wants me to learn how to worship Him. The Father "seeks those who will worship Him in spirit and truth" (John 4:23).

Worship is a mysterious concept. It is not the same as praise. It involves humility, brokenness, submission, sacrifice, and adoration. It is an attitude of the heart that can only be attained in the power of Holy Spirit. It is not easy to learn how to worship God as a lifestyle, but that is the goal: to live in a constant attitude of worship. Developing this lifestyle of unbroken worship begins with learning how to be in His presence alone and learn to love being with Him alone.

When love consumes the heart, only the object of that love can satisfy the heart. God loves us perfectly. He is satisfied when He has us completely to Himself, because we are the object of His perfect love. He is honored and glorified when we trust and obey Him, but He is most pleased when we will settle for nothing less than knowing His heart. The jealous yearning of the Holy Spirit in the believer is to fall in love with the heart of God (James 4:5), to have a divine Holy Spirit love in us that consumes us and drives everything else out of our heart that competes for our attention. He merits and wants our total devotion. "You shall have no other gods before me" (Exodus 20:3) is the heart of His desire.

I mentioned earlier that my knowledge of the Bible had become a god. A god is anything that gives me what I think I need or want, such as completeness, status, pleasure, satisfaction, fulfillment, security, escape, position, confidence, recognition, and acceptance. There is one thing that a little "g" god cannot give us that we desperately desire, and that is forgiveness and peace with God (Romans 5:1). We allow ourselves to be deceived by all those other things listed above, thinking they will make us happy. We seek them in a thousand different ways. Even mature believers fall into this trap of deception. It takes us a long time to learn that *He* is the only *One* Who can satisfy the deep longings of our heart (John 10:10).

As I began the first few weeks of giving my first hour to the Lord, I made some discoveries. He wanted me to be with Him just for Him. It was okay to ask Him for things, but that is not

The Wind That Never Changes

the main reason I was there. It was so He could have me completely to Himself. I even ran a fan in the room so I would not be distracted by noises elsewhere in the house. I realized that I could not give this kind of undivided attention to Him if I were doing anything else like driving, jogging, riding an exercise bike, etc. There is nothing wrong with using such times to pray, but it is not the same. He wanted my total attention.

As time went on I noticed I had a lot of problems with thoughts popping into my mind. I struggled with this for days and asked Him about it. His reply came quite unexpectedly one morning as I was getting ready for work: "You have an undisciplined mind." I wondered what that meant. The first thing I learned about having a more disciplined mind was the discovery that the thoughts that troubled me in the morning often were from what I was doing the day before. If I watched an intense action movie or some other activity that ordinarily I would not consider harmful, it was hard to clear my mind the next day. Therefore, I started being more careful about what I did or even allowed myself to think. As time went on I became better at bringing all the thoughts captive and was able to be in His presence without distracting thoughts.

After a few months I began to notice another occurrence. When I would start my time with Him, I would just kneel quietly and calm my mind and heart. Often I would meditate on His love or other attributes. Sometimes I would read a psalm or sing a song quietly. My desire was to focus on Him as much as I could. Sometimes something would happen that I cannot explain. It seems as if I was able to enter into a deeper place where He was more real. I would weep for joy, sometimes laugh in delight, or just bow in wonder and awe. It was as if He were allowing me to know His presence with me, and it was wonderfully overwhelming. It is like a mountain-top experience, something that transcends the physical realm. At such a moment you know you are in contact with Him and Him with you. You are totally lost in His love, power, grace, and beauty. You are consumed with God. Nothing else matters.

I also made a discovery one morning in the middle of one of these times: As I worshiped Him I wanted to confess my sin because I felt so unworthy. When I started to confess my sin it was as if He withdrew. This happened on several occasions. One thing I added to my daily routine was to make sure I was "confessed-up" as it were before my morning time with Him. I was to realize later that during these Holy times with Him, it is not about me in any way. Even confessing my sins involves taking my attention off Him and placing it on me. I could never predict when He would give me one of those special times, nor could I make it happen.

On many a morning I would go in depressed, sad, discouraged, or some other negative emotion due to the stress of life, and He would manifest Himself to me. It was as if I would become another person and leave the room totally joyful. I still had all those problems, but they were in a completely different perspective. As time went on, I was surprised how often that would happen. I don't want to give the impression that every morning was wonderful. Many mornings my time with Him was like eating oatmeal with nothing but water—nourishing, but not very tasty. However, my whole life revolved around my time in the morning with Him, and it became my highest priority. It had become the foundation of my daily walk with God. My desire was to give Him my best, to honor Him every morning by giving myself to Him without any other distraction.

As this was happening to me, I began to teach it to my congregation. I emphasized how important it was to seek God for God alone. One of the ladies in our church took my admonition to heart. She began seeking God every morning from 2:00 till 3:00 am. This was just the way she felt led to do it. She did this for six months every day and did not tell anyone. One Sunday morning she came in radiant. He had manifested Himself to her as I had been sharing about. She was joyful beyond words. For some reason as she sought the Lord every morning for six months, He was not pleased to manifest Himself to her until now. She confessed that the joy of knowing Him deeper was so completely satisfying and thrilling that she considered the six months she had to wait nothing in comparison with the joy that she now had. I share her story by way of illustration and encouragement "that we will reap if we faint not" (Galatians 6:9).

I don't know how we change when we draw near to God. The scripture says as we gaze on Him, we are transformed into His image by the Holy Spirit (II Corinthians 3:18). The one who knows me best noticed a significant change after about a year. I am not even sure what she noticed or how I changed. I do know that my sensitivity to sin was greatly enhanced, and the "bar" for holiness was raised a lot. Some things I thought or did before I started spending time with Him that did not bother me, now bothered me. I also was not aware that I was different. She saw it, but I did not.

About this time, I began to notice that my wife was starting to love me in a different way. She had always loved me, but something was different. I don't know any other way to say it. She adored me. I did not then or now deserve how she loves and esteems me. Over the years this effect seemed to spread to others. They would esteem me in a way I knew I did not deserve. People wanted to be with me, and I could not figure out why. Don't they know how weak and sinful I am? At this point in my life I would freely tell them in detail of my weaknesses, but it seemed to make no difference. They still wanted to be with me.

I know the explanation, even though I don't understand it or how it works: Being with Jesus every morning somehow has abounded to Him being manifest in my life that others see and I do not. Another byproduct of getting closer to Jesus is awareness of your own sin. I am probably holier in my daily life than I have ever been. Yet the sin and imperfections that remain in my heart loom so large that I am not always aware I have made any progress in holiness.

There are two more observations I want to make. As I discussed earlier, insecurity has been a constant companion all my life. It peaked the first few years I was married. It is not rational, and I don't defend how I felt. I always struggled with believing I was a bum. In fact, for years I wanted to win a Nobel Prize in physics so the world would know I was not a loser. It doesn't matter what everybody else thinks of me. What matters is how I see myself. For most of my life I have seen myself as a loser. To this day, when I go to family reunions, all my cousins call me the loser name I had as a child. Consequently, I have always had to fight feelings of inadequacy or of not being good enough, no matter what I accomplished. In fact, even if I had won the Nobel Prize, that would not have solved the problem.

After a few years of seeking the Lord for Himself as I have described, I discovered that the insecurity in my heart was greatly reduced. I cannot say it was completely gone. However, it was so much less that it made an impression. Now, after over eleven years of seeking Him, I am even more secure. I finally really like myself in the best sense. I don't think it is pride, but rather contentment. I am content to be me. I don't want to be different except in my desire to be more like Jesus. It is wonderfully liberating. I think what happens is when we really get to know Jesus and His love, we find that is all we ever really wanted. He accepts me and loves me like I am. I am secure in His love.

The second observation I want to make seems contradictory, but it is not. While I am very secure in His love, I find that without Him I am wretched. I really, really know that in me is no good thing. We all believe this theoretically or theologically but don't really believe it practically. If we did, pride would never be a problem. Along with this is the realization that anything good that comes out of my life is from Jesus. As I said earlier, pride never goes away completely, and the flesh nature is just as corrupt as ever. As we grow in the grace and knowledge of Him, we realize, as He said, that apart from Him we can do nothing (John 15:5).

After my first year of seeking God and God alone, my wife began to be convicted to do the same thing. She has had identical results. All her life she was insecure, but for different reasons than mine. As she invested time in her relationship with her

Lord and Savior every day, she started changing, and I could see it. It is interesting to note that her experience with God is different from mine in that she had her quiet time at a different time during the day. Her personality is different from mine. I am naturally emotional and passionate. My wife is much more reserved and quiet spoken. In time, however, the result was the same. Jesus let her know Him in a way that she never had. She learned to weep and worship before Him in joy and brokenness. Over the years as she has continued to seek Him as her first priority, she confesses Jesus has set her free from her insecurities.

By January of 2003, when we had our thirty-third anniversary, I had been spending time with the Lord every morning for over three years. It was at this point in our journey that He had her tell me what I had been waiting to hear for twenty years. This completes the story of my twenty-year wait for my wife to tell me, "Your love has set me free." Yet, I am still learning to love my wife. The next section discusses the greatest lesson my wife and I are learning in life and how it allows us to have an "eternal life" marriage.

Jesus Is Enough

It is a sad but true observation of human nature that we think we know what is best for us. A baby less than a year old regularly manifests frustration with its parents when the parents do something the baby doesn't like or understand. So many things the baby thinks he can do or he wants to do are harmful. When the parents wisely intervene, the baby does not like it and vents his displeasure. Such is the human condition. We live our entire life thinking our way is best. Our darkened human nature dictates to us what we think will make us happy. We look for significance, acceptance, fulfillment, peace, and happiness in all the wrong places. Surely someone loving us will make us happy. Surely success in some form will make us happy. Surely something will fill this deep, compelling desire in our being.

God is the parent, and we are like the babies. The first problem with this analogy is that the difference between us and God is far greater than the difference between loving, wise parents and a baby one-year-old. The baby cannot realize or accept the parents' control because he only knows what he has learned in the first twelve months of his life. Self-centeredness is programed into the baby. He only cares about what he needs and wants. This is fine for a baby. The task of the parents is to help the baby come to see that life is not about himself. The parents have lived enough years to experience life's realities and hopefully learn lessons about sacrifice, serving, patience, and basically putting other's needs, in this case the baby, above their own. Their primary motivation is love. They want their baby to feel loved and secure, and have the best life that they can provide.

What does God want for His babies, human beings redeemed by the blood of Jesus? He wants the same things. He wants us to know His love and His care, and to experience the very best, most fulfilling life possible. The problem is that none of His babies knows what such a life looks like or how to get there. Think about the young baby: Does the baby have any clue as to how he grows into a mature, fulfilled adult? Not only does the baby not have any clue, he is not capable of understanding what it looks like or feels like to be grown up. The parents do, because they are mature. Because of this they are far better qualified to guide the baby and provide the nurturing circumstances—many of which the baby won't like or understand—to help the baby experience and learn the lessons necessary for a happy life. If the baby is allowed to make up his own rules without the guidance of loving, wise parents, he will grow up to be a self-centered adult and never know fulfillment or joy.

The second problem with the parent/baby analogy as it relates to the God/human relationship is that humans are eternal beings with a God-given spirit. We say this as something we know or have been taught, but we really don't know what it means. Why are people fundamentally different from all the other animals, or are they? There are books written trying to define what is unique about humans, but not everyone agrees that there really is a difference between humans and animals. Some argue that the difference is only in degrees of attributes like intelligence and emotions. If it is true that humans are not fundamentally different from animals, don't have an eternal spirit, and are not eternal beings that will exist forever, then the whole discussion is pointless. Life is just a chance existence with no direction or purpose, and humans are products of natural, physical processes, and are orphans.

However, if God really did create the heavens and the earth and everything in them, and humans really are unique beings created in His image with an eternal spirit, then the most important goals in life should be to find out why we are here, what we are to do, and where we are going? Humans have been trying to figure out the answers to these questions as long as there have been humans. Remember the earlier discussion on the baby—how he was incapable of knowing what it is like to be a mature adult? The same problem is true here. As humans, we are incapable of understanding what we are to become as eternal beings. None of us, except One, has ever been in the eternal realm. How can we possibly know what circumstances can best prepare us for eternity when we can't understand eternity?

Every religion in the world, historically and today, including many branches of Christianity, has a recipe for pleasing God that includes good works that must be done. Human understanding of eternity and how to gain eternity always includes earning it in some way. Therefore, every religion has a formula of behavior that somehow wins God's approval and earns the penitent seeker a place in heaven. The real way to eternity is so foreign to human nature that no human would ever think of it. It does not make sense to human nature. Go back to the one-year-old baby. Would the baby understand or be able to articulate self-sacrifice? Would the baby know the life circumstances and experiences that will lead to an understanding of self-sacrifice and how it works in relationships? This is the essence of love. The parents are showing loving self-sacrifice to the baby countless times a day, but it will be years before the baby understands what the parents are doing and why, probably not until the baby has its own baby. The parent/baby relationship is not about what the baby can do for the parents, but rather what the parents do for the baby.

It is so natural for human reason to turn our relationship with God into a collection of rules that stipulate what is correct to do or not do in order to please God. Superficially, this makes everything neat and predictable. If you do all the right things, you can earn God's approval and salvation. If you do the wrong things, you go to eternal punishment. Sadly, this is the way most people see religion and even Christianity. Just like the parent/baby analogy, it is not about what we can do for God, but about believing and receiving what He has done for us. Only the Holy Spirit can reveal to a human heart how biblical salvation really works (Galatians 1:12).

In Romans 14:17 Paul reminds us that the kingdom of God is not about religious activity, but about righteousness, peace, and joy that can only come from God the Holy Spirit. Righteousness means so much more than just doing what is right all the time and not doing what is wrong. Righteousness is the Holy life of God Himself given to the repentant, believing, receiving sinner (II Corinthians 5:21). The Gift of the righteousness of Jesus Himself was purchased by His blood on the cross. The first benefit is that when God looks at one of His redeemed children, He sees the perfect righteousness of His Holy Son, Jesus, and He no longer sees our sin because Jesus took it away by becoming our sacrifice for sin. Therefore, we have peace with God and are no longer under His wrath (Romans 5:1). But, being holy in the sight of God, is just the beginning of the benefits of His righteousness. His Holy life imparted by the Holy Spirit shows us how to live for His glory. He not only shows us how to live, but also gives us the power to do things we could not do on our own. He gives us a divine love that is redemptive

The Wind That Never Changes

(Romans 5:5). This divine, redemptive love affects every relationship we have in our entire life. My first taste of this divine love was that night in the rescue mission. It was an instant transformation of my heart from self-centered to Christ-centered. Living a life in the power of divine love leads to peace and joy that cannot be described (I Peter 1:8).

Biblical salvation leads to a real, dynamic, living relationship with God. It is complex, as is any relationship between two intelligent beings. Like any relationship, it must be nurtured and developed. It involves fellowship and mutual communication. God revealing Himself to His child is His will (John 14:21). *Experiencing God in daily living is the normal Christian life.*

From Genesis to Revelation, the Bible reveals that God's provision for every need of the human heart is Jesus. This sounds simple, but it is not. It takes a lifetime to begin to learn what this means. We think we know what it means, but our behavior demonstrates otherwise. Anytime we are discouraged, depressed, fearful, proud, unforgiving, selfish, angry, covetous, discontent, impatient, and a host of similar negative emotions, it shows we do not know that Jesus is Enough. It shows we want something more than Jesus to make us happy, secure, peaceful, content, or whatever. This is an insult to God! God created us and knows us like we do not know ourselves. He knows what will make us fulfilled, and we do not. It would never occur to us that having a relationship with Jesus is what we really need and want. It would never occur to us that we are incapable of entering into a relationship with Jesus without God's help. He has to do it (John 6:44; Ephesians 2:8–10). Until we humble ourselves and admit our inability to please God on our own, we will never understand His Salvation. Pride is the greatest barrier in the human heart to the grace of God. Like the baby, we think we know best.

Several years ago, my son-in-law became severely ill and went from perfect health to eternity in six days. He died from septic shock, which is bacteria in the blood. We never found out why it happened. He was thirty-four years old, a devoted Christian, husband of my daughter, father of three small children, principal of a Christian school, and in his third year of graduate school for his doctorate. In six surreal days we watched him die. Thousands of Christians were praying for him. His funeral was one of the largest in recent memory in our community. He was loved and respected by many. Our lives were suddenly turned upside down. It seemed my daughter's perfect life was over. They had been married for ten years and had a wonderful relationship. What was she to do? She spent hours alone and seemed to be in a fog. We prayed and served her and our three grandchildren as best we could. Sometime after her husband's death she started coming out of the fog. She said, "Daddy, *Jesus is enough*." She had come to realize that she still had the Source of everything joyful in her life. Yes, her beloved husband was gone. But she realized the love they had shared for those ten years was from Jesus, and she still had that love.

Jesus is enough. After my daughter said that to me, I decided to make it my personal tagline or motto. I had a bumper sticker made for my car. In addition to "Jesus is Enough" the bumper sticker has a scripture reference, Psalm 73:25:

> Whom have I in heaven but thee? And there is none upon earth that I desire besides thee.

This verse sums up the matter. Jesus is our Advocate in heaven before the Father. His blood shed on the cross for our sins paid the full price for our complete redemption. His resurrection life in us gives us the power by the indwelling Holy Spirit to live a Godly life that we could not live on our own power. Jesus is all I need to get to heaven. Compared to Jesus, there is nothing on earth that can make me complete, fulfilled, and happy, or however we want to say it. He is my first love. Whatever comes my way, if Jesus is not in it, I don't want it. He and He alone can satisfy my heart.

It is a sad but true observation that people who are abused can turn out to be abusers; hurt people hurt people. In the same way, people who have responded to the love and grace of God can help others respond to the love and grace of God. God's love is redemptive. It sets us free from the crippling power of self. Self does not know what it wants. It seeks gratification in so many ways, as has been discussed. Jesus said that His disciples must learn to deny self. This is not easy to do, especially if what we are seeking appears to be good, like success in a career or ministry. It took years for me to realize that things I thought were good to pursue were actually bad. I was trying to satisfy things in my heart that only Jesus can satisfy. The book of James calls this spiritual adultery (James 4:4). It is also called having other gods before the one and only God (Exodus 20: 2–3). Until I allow Jesus to deal with and set me free from pride, insecurity, fear, ambition, greed, and selfishness, His redemptive love cannot be manifest in my life. We are not really free until we learn to live Psalm 73:25. Jesus said, "If the Son sets you free, you will be free indeed" (John 8:36). If we want to love anyone like Jesus loves us, it must be redemptive love, love that sets us free from the bondage of sin and self. We cannot love like that until we have allowed Jesus to love us and set us free.

My wife is free by my love because I have become free in His love. She finds peace in my eyes because I have found peace in His eyes (Song of Solomon 8:10).

Eternal Life Marriage

The title for this final section may seem a little strange. The reason I use this title is that God has given my wife and me the gift of eternal life in Jesus Christ. God's intent is that we grow in learning how to allow His life, eternal life, to be manifested in everything we do. Eternal life is a quality of life, not just duration of life. It is the kind of life that we receive when we truly come to know Jesus as our Savior, Lord, and Life.

When my wife and I give the seminar on marriage, we call the series of seven lessons, "In The Garden." We point out that God wants us to live life in His presence like Adam and Eve before the fall. Our goal is to be in constant communion with God and to eat from the Tree of Life, which is Jesus. He is our "daily bread." The first lesson in learning to have an eternal life marriage is to realize that our relationship as husband and wife is directly a result of our personal, individual relationships with Jesus. *We are learning that our marriage is only as good as our individual walks with Jesus.* It takes both of us seeking Him with our whole heart every day. We have noticed that when either one of us is not giving priority to Jesus, our marriage relationship suffers. While this story has been about specifics of my journey, my wife has had similar experiences and revelations. She seeks the presence of God every day, as I do, and has discovered the , satisfying, liberating joy of knowing Him. We have both learned, "*If you are not satisfied with Jesus, you will not be satisfied with anything.*"

We all approach life with expectations. These expectations are formed from our genetics and life experiences, but mostly from our spiritual condition. Sadly, we allow our darkened, sinful nature to dictate what we think will make us happy. Since this nature is rooted in selfishness, which is contrary to the nature of God, happiness can never happen. Jesus said, "I am come that they may have life, and have life it in abundance" (John 10:10). As discussed in the previous section, God knows that nothing but He can make us happy. He loves us too much to allow us to find fulfillment in any other place or thing. These are the little "g" gods. My wife and I have learned that we cannot give each other what only God can give us. We do not look to each other for happiness, completeness, or anything else. When we each find our total joy in Jesus our Life, it sets us free to love each other in a redemptive way. That is, love each other with the Holy Spirit's supernatural love (Romans 5:5). All the events I have shared in this story are nothing more than God's dealings with me in learning to walk in the Spirit rather than my old sinful nature. It has taken a lifetime and, I am still learning.

So what does an eternal life marriage look like? For my wife and me, it is living in the deep places of our hearts together. My

The Wind That Never Changes

wife and I often speak of a place in our hearts that we refer to as *holy ground*. It is that deep place where all our fears and hopes reside, a place that no one else sees or knows about. We guard that part of our being because revealing what is there makes us vulnerable, exposed, and emotionally naked. For us, it is learning to live intimately in the holy ground of each other's heart.

Can anyone love and accept me if they knew what I was really like in the deep places of my heart? This is a good question. My wife and I spent the first thirty years of our marriage learning to connect with each other from "deep unto deep" (Psalm 42:7). For the first eleven years of our marriage there were problems that existed between us that were too painful to discuss, so we didn't. God had to heal a lot of emotional and spiritual wounds in both of us before we were secure and mature enough to begin becoming one in the deep places of our hearts. This is the major difference that we have found in "eternal life" marriage. *We continually live in the depths of each other's heart.* We connect regularly in the deepest aspect of our being. The deep place is both strong and fragile. It is the place of our character and also the place of greatest tenderness.

We have learned not to carelessly walk into each other's holy place with "spiked shoes." We take off our spiked shoes of anger, criticism, insensitivity, pride, superiority, un-forgiveness, grudge holding, and even expectation. We come into each other's hearts with one motive and one motive alone: to love. Love means unconditional acceptance, putting your spouse above yourself, no expectations, forgiveness, delight, and honor. With this attitude, we can share our deepest thoughts. Nothing is held back or hidden. We explore together our weaknesses, fears, and dreams. Often one of us will say, "I need to confess something, but I am ashamed." Even though we are ashamed, the unconditional love and acceptance we show each other makes it possible to confess to each other without fear. We have both found that the power of the oppressive thought or feeling is broken when it is brought out into the light. We call it "getting it on the table." Drag it out of the deep place and look at it for what it is. It is very liberating to have such a relationship. Interestingly, the more honest and real we are with each other, the more we love and respect each other.

This deep relationship and communication between us takes constant nurturing. We have both found that sometimes the frantic demands of daily life dull the sweetness of our oneness. As mentioned earlier, if each of us does not daily nurture our relationship with our Heavenly Father through our Lord Jesus in the power of the Holy Spirit, our marriage relationship suffers. This cannot be emphasized enough. The secret of eternal life marriage is both husband and wife having a living, vibrant, real, daily walk with God our Father through Jesus Christ our Lord and Savior in the power of the Holy Spirit. Our relationship with Jesus takes priority over our relationship with each other. The passion of our relationship with God is reflected in our relationship with each other. We keep each other on a short leash when it comes to encouraging each other in Godliness. Almost daily one of us says to the other one, "Something's wrong." This means that she has detected unsettledness in my spirit that is affecting our relationship. I may not even be aware that anything is wrong in my heart. Since she knows me so well, it doesn't take much wrong in me for her to notice, and the same goes for my sensitivity to her spirit. We watch over each other. The sweetness of our relationship is so precious and enjoyable that we both are attuned to anything that brings even the slightest disruption.

As you read this you might be tempted to say, "Don't you each have a life? Have you lost your individual identity?" Well, in a sense we have lost our individual identities. We each want to be like Jesus as much as we can. Perfection is never possible in this life. Both of us fall regularly. However, as one song goes, "We fall down, we get up, we fall down, and we get up" (1). As we individually seek daily to fall more in love with Jesus, we find ourselves falling more in love with each other. As we seek His kingdom and righteousness first *above all other things*, including our individual selves and each other, we each find a power and liberating joy that fills the rest of our lives with His presence. Our relationships with our families, friends, co-workers, and everything else in our lives are touched by Divine eternal life that flows out of us without our even being aware of it. Others are regularly drawn to us and they don't even know why. Our marriage is like a drinking cup full of water. When a person is thirsty for water, they are not too concerned about the cup as long as it is clean and the water is clean. Jesus is the clean, clear Water of Life. My wife and I contain this water, the Holy Spirit. Our desire is to be a clean, holy cup so others can drink that water.

When we are willing to make the necessary investment it takes to daily seek Jesus first in our lives, we find an amazing return. Remember, we don't seek Jesus first for the return. *We seek Jesus first for Jesus*. He takes care of the return. Sometimes He takes years. God does not work like we do. His ways are not like ours. They are unimaginably better. This is called walking by faith and not sight. It can only be done in the power of the Holy Spirit.

I like to tell people, "I keep my wife in her place." They look at me kind of funny until I tell them what kind of place: "On a pedestal with me adoring her." She keeps me in the same place, Glory to God!

NOTE:

1. Kyle David Matthews, "We Fall Down," (Universal, 1997).

Made in the USA
Lexington, KY
30 June 2019